Win life in 100 pages.

A Journey to Self-Discovery and Personal Growth

“A body without mind is like a bird without wings.”

Tizil Yadav

SPI PUBLICATIONS

Published by **SPI Publications**, www.spipublications.in
SPI, the **SPI logo**, and **Split Poetry India** are trademarks of **SPI Publications**, or its affiliates.
ISBN-13: 978-81-992622-8-7

First Edition 2025

SPI Publications

Corporate & Editorial Office

117/2, Sector 37, Khandsa Road,
Gurgaon, Haryana 122 001
Phone: +91 98355 52940
Email: contact@spipublications.in
Website: www.spipublications.in

Processed and Printed in India

Introduction:

In a world overflowing with noise and distractions, finding the time and space to truly connect with ourselves can feel like a daunting task. Yet, the path to self-discovery is one of the most rewarding journeys we can undertake. It's a journey that leads not only to understanding our minds but also to uncovering the true potential that lies within us. This book, "***Win life in 100 pages***" is inspired by my own experiences and challenges. It's a guide designed to help you explore the depths of your mind, offering practical insights, wisdom, and steps to embrace your authentic self. As you turn these pages, you'll embark on a transformative journey towards personal growth, clarity, and lasting inner peace.

Preface

Life is an unpredictable journey, filled with hurdles and hardships that test our resilience, strength, and determination. As I reflect on my own experiences, I offer my deepest gratitude to life itself—not for its ease but for its challenges. These challenges became my greatest teachers, shaping my mindset, igniting my passion, and inspiring me to pen this book: *Win Life in 100 Pages*.

Have you ever felt overwhelmed by your surroundings? Have you ever doubted your inner strength or underestimated your potential? Have you faced moments when your mind seemed to hit its limits, leaving you uncertain about the future? If your answer is yes, then this book is for you. Through its pages, I aim to provide not just answers but also practical tools to navigate life's toughest moments and emerge victorious.

This book is a culmination of personal stories, hard-learned lessons, and transformative strategies. It draws inspiration from my journey—from overcoming a debilitating back injury to rediscovering joy, discipline, and purpose. You will learn how to harness the power of meditation to clear your mind, use writing as a tool for self-reflection, and visualize success even when the odds seem stacked against you. You'll uncover methods to earn more, rekindle happiness, and remain focused on your ultimate goals despite distractions and doubts.

Every chapter is designed to inspire action and spark change. The aim is simple: to help you unlock your potential and win at life. Whether you are struggling with motivation, discipline, or simply need a fresh perspective, this book will guide you toward creating the life you desire.

So, take a deep breath, turn the page, and embark on this journey to win life in just 100 pages.

Contents

Chapter 1

What is the potential of your mind!

"Mind is the wing of the human."

Tizilyadav

The mind is a powerful yet often misunderstood tool. While most people recognize its potential, few truly harness it. Many are trapped in a cycle of negative thinking, unable to break free and achieve their goals. Through my experiences and research, I've realized that mastering the mind requires both patience and strategy. In this chapter, I will explore how to manage the mind effectively, using personal anecdotes, practical strategies, and insights into spirituality as a tool to combat overthinking, depression, and anxiety.

The Power of the Mind

Let's start with a question: *How many of you know the true potential of your mind?* My answer: very few, if any. The majority of people are unable to defeat the negative thoughts that dominate their minds. Instead of taking charge, they let their minds control them.

Another question: *How many of you spend too much time talking and procrastinating?* If your answer is yes, it's time to reevaluate your priorities. Excessive talking often reflects a lack of focus and discipline, indicating a disconnection from one's goals. My words may seem harsh, but if you continue reading, they will guide you toward achieving inner peace and clarity.

The Role of Manifestation and Wisdom

Many self-help books highlight the importance of changing our thinking patterns, yet few provide actionable methods to achieve this. For instance, in *Think Straight* by Darius Foroux, the author discusses linear thinking and mistrusting the mind. While these ideas are valuable, they don't fully explain how to escape the "prison" of our thoughts.

From my experience, we don't need to escape our minds. Instead, we need to nurture them like infants—offering care, patience, and understanding.

Personal Anecdote: Lessons from a Solo Shrine Journey

One of the most profound lessons I learned came during a solo trip to *Maa Vaishno Devi*, a holy shrine located 5,200 feet above sea level in the Trikuta Mountains of Katra, Jammu. During this journey, I lost my bag, which contained my wallet, charger, clothes, journal, and other essentials. Alone in a strange city, without money or internet access, I faced a choice: panic or remain calm.

I chose calmness. I treated my mind with patience, focusing on enjoying the journey rather than dwelling on the loss. The breathtaking mountains and serene atmosphere reminded me to live in the moment. This experience taught me that the mind's natural tendency to spiral into chaos can be overcome with deliberate effort and positive reinforcement.

How to Treat the Mind

We often scold or criticize ourselves when things go wrong. Instead, we should treat our minds as we would a child. Here's how:

- **Gentle Reasoning:** When a child wants something harmful, we don't deny them outright. Instead, we explain gently why it's not good for them. Similarly, when negative thoughts arise, reason with your mind rather than suppressing or ignoring those thoughts

- **Positive Distraction:** Redirect your mind to constructive activities, such as journaling, meditation, or creative pursuits.

The Role of Spirituality

Spirituality offers profound tools for managing the mind. Whether you believe in a higher power or not, spiritual practices can provide a framework for navigating life's challenges. For example:

1. **Faith and Trust:** Believing that a higher power will guide you can instill a sense of peace and reduce overthinking.

2. **Mind Tricks:** Even skeptics can use the concept of a higher power as a mental tool to stay calm and grounded during difficult times.

The Echoes of Silence

Life had become a relentless blur, my thoughts an overwhelming tide. After my brother's accident, fear settled deep, amplifying every whisper of anxiety. I withdrew into silence, unable to tame the chaos in my mind.

One sleepless night, the weight of time pressed hard on me. But then I realized: "We cannot control the time, but the rhythm can be controlled." I started with small steps—organizing my room, walking outside, and taking slow, deliberate breaths. Each act, no matter how minor, began to align my inner rhythm.

The hours didn't change their pace, but I did. Slowly, the silence I dreaded became a space for calm. By adjusting my rhythm, I found a way to live alongside time, rather than fighting it.

The Illusion of Desire

The mind's fundamental nature is to desire. If you have a home, you want a car. If you have a car, you want a luxury vehicle. While ambition can drive growth, unchecked desire can create stress and dissatisfaction.

This endless cycle of wanting is what I call *the illusion*. While it motivates us to achieve more, it also traps us in a state of perpetual discontent. In upcoming chapters, I'll explore ways to balance ambition and contentment.

Final Thoughts

The mind is not an enemy to be defeated but an ally to be nurtured. Treat it with care, and it will guide you toward clarity and peace. By understanding the nature of overthinking, depression, and anxiety, and by embracing spirituality and mindfulness, you can unlock the mind's true potential.

Stay tuned for future chapters, where we'll dive deeper into the concept of illusions and strategies to conquer them. Let's embark on this journey together to transform our minds and lives.

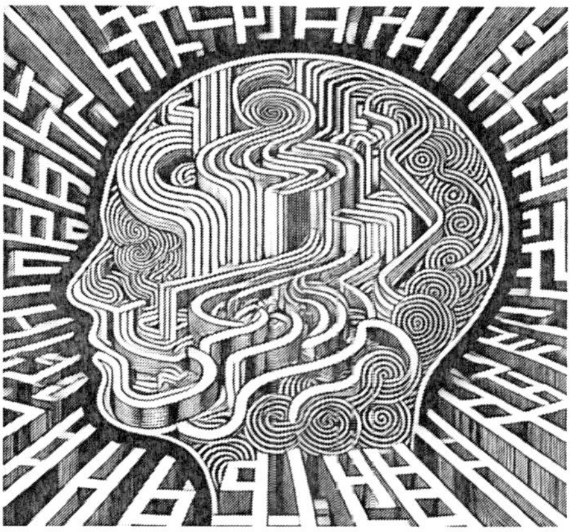

Chapter-2

The Language of Emotion

"Own your mind, Don't let emotions govern your thoughts"

tizil yadav

Introduction: What Are Emotions?
Emotions are an inherent part of human existence. Despite being universal, emotions are complex and often difficult to define. Over time, several definitions have emerged:

- Some describe emotions as *"conscious mental reactions"* that involve physiological changes.

- Others highlight emotions as *"feelings, passions, and sentiments."*

One of the most insightful perspectives comes from **Joseph LeDoux**, a prominent American neuroscientist. He defines emotions as *"the result of a cognitive and conscious process,"* emphasizing their connection to the brain's intricate functions. In his influential book, *The Emotional Brain* (1972), LeDoux asked an intriguing question: *"Is emotion our first fear?"*

The answer, based on evolutionary psychology, is likely yes. Fear is considered one of the first emotions to evolve, playing a vital role in survival by alerting humans to danger. However, in modern times, fear often manifests in non-life-threatening situations, such as academic performance, relationships, or personal ambitions.

In the context of emotions, fear plays a significant role in how many people approach spirituality and religion. For some, fear is not just limited to worldly concerns but extends to their relationship with God. Just as fear can motivate individuals to avoid harmful consequences in everyday life, it can also drive people to worship God out of fear of divine punishment, misfortune, or the uncertainty of the afterlife.

The Role of Fear in Our Lives

Fear, while initially a protective mechanism, can either motivate or paralyze us. It influences our decisions and behaviors, often in subtle ways.

- **Fear of Consequences**: Fear can guide individuals to make better choices. For instance:

    - A student attends classes regularly to avoid low attendance affecting their grades.

    - A gym-goer might skip leg day, fearing the pain of delayed onset muscle soreness.

- **Personal Example: A Nightmare of Loss**
  During a challenging phase of my life, I experienced a recurring nightmare in which my mother died in a car accident. This nightmare left me emotionally shaken, especially because I deeply love my mother. At the time, I was struggling with depression, which magnified my fears and made even minor stressors overwhelming.

- **Fear of Failure**
  When I began writing my first book, I was consumed by fear:
    - *What if my content isn't good enough?*
    - *What if readers don't appreciate my work?*

This fear could have stopped me, but I chose to confront it and found a way forward.

Steps to Overcome Fear

Overcoming fear is not easy, but it is achievable with deliberate actions and mindset shifts. Here are the steps I took:

1. Take the First Step

The first step toward addressing fear is often the hardest. When I started writing my book, my fears evaporated as soon as I began. Taking action transforms fear from a looming threat into a manageable task.

2. Confront Fear Head-On

Ask yourself:

- *What is causing this fear?*
- *Why am I scared?*
- *How can I address it?*

  By analyzing the root cause of your fear, you can devise practical solutions and build confidence.

3. Practice Self-Love

Self-love is essential. By prioritizing your emotional and mental well-being, you create a foundation for resilience. Caring for your inner self enables you to approach challenges with clarity and strength.

4. Engage in Physical Activity

Physical exercise, especially team sports or endurance-based activities, triggers the release of **endorphins**—hormones that improve mood and reduce stress. These activities not only enhance physical health but also foster mental resilience.

Wisdom from the Bhagavad Gita

The teachings of the *Shree Bhagavad Gita* offer profound insights into emotions and fear. In **Chapter 2, Verse 14**, Lord Krishna advises Arjuna:
"O son of Kunti, the nonpermanent appearance of happiness and distress, and their disappearance in due course, are like the appearance and disappearance of winter and summer seasons. They arise from sense perception, and one must learn to tolerate them without being disturbed."

This verse highlights the impermanence of emotions like fear and anxiety, encouraging us to tolerate life's dualities with equanimity. Krishna's wisdom serves as a reminder that fear, like happiness and distress, is fleeting.

Strategies for Mind Mastery

Mastering emotions requires understanding the mind's workings. Here are practical strategies:

1. Gentle Self-Treatment

Treat your mind as you would a child—gently redirecting it when it strays. When fear arises, acknowledge it and guide your thoughts toward constructive solutions.

2. Faith and Perspective

Faith in a higher power or universal order can provide comfort during challenging times. For instance, during a pilgrimage to *Maa Vaishno Devi*, I lost my belongings but remained calm, trusting the journey's purpose. Even for non-believers, adopting a mindset of acceptance can help ease fear.

3. Overcoming Emotional Challenges

Three common emotional hurdles include:

- **Overthinking**: Repetitive thoughts that create mental paralysis.
- **Depression**: Lingering distress from past incidents.
- **Anxiety**: Fear of uncertain future events.

Mindfulness practices, self-reflection, and physical activities can help address these challenges effectively.

Conclusion: Emotions as Tools for Growth

Fear, though often perceived negatively, is a natural and necessary emotion. When approached with self-awareness and the right strategies, fear can become a catalyst for growth and resilience. By taking deliberate steps—starting small, confronting fear, practicing self-love, and staying active—you can transform fear into a source of strength.

As highlighted in the *Shree Bhagavad Gita*, the key is to recognize the impermanence of fear and other emotions, embracing them as part of life's ever-changing journey. In future chapters, we'll explore additional strategies and examples to help you navigate the intricate world of emotions with confidence and clarity.

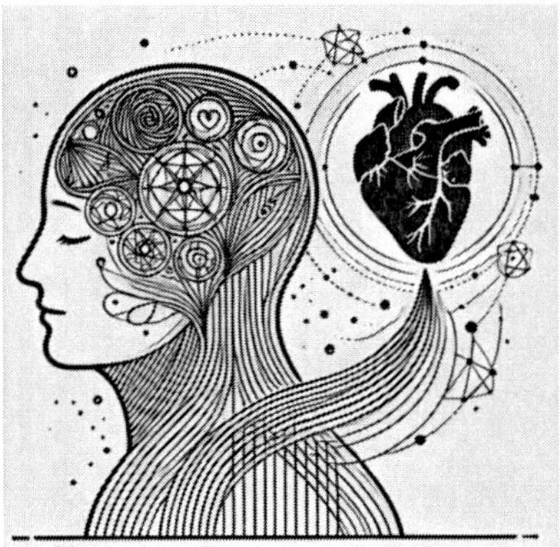

CHAPTER— 3

The Layers of Mind

"Let it Go, and the heaviness Fades"

by tizilyadav

Everyone talks about the philosophy of making small, incremental changes in life, but rarely does anyone explain what those changes should be or how to take those first steps. In this chapter, I aim to provide you with practical steps to help you navigate through the maze of life—a maze that often leaves us trapped, confused, and uncertain about the right path forward.

Every individual faces unique challenges, but there are commonalities in the phases of life that we all go through. Drawing inspiration from Vedic philosophy, let's explore the four fundamental activities that humans and animals share:

1. Eating (Āhāra)

Food sustains life for both humans and animals. When you prepare meals at home or purchase groceries, you fulfill the same essential need as a dog eagerly awaiting its meal. Eating is not just a biological necessity; it's a reminder of the simple, shared act of sustaining life.

2. Sleeping (Nidrā)

Rest rejuvenates the body and mind for both humans and animals. Whether it's you sleeping after a long day or a cat curling up for hours, sleep is vital to recovery from physical and mental exertion. It's a shared necessity that restores balance.

3. Mating (Maithuna)

The instinct to reproduce is universal. Humans form bonds, create families, and build relationships, just as animals instinctively procreate and form connections for survival. Whether it's a pair of birds building a nest or a couple starting a family, this natural instinct drives life forward.

4. Defending (Bhaya or Rakṣā)

Both humans and animals engage in self-preservation. You might install a security system at home, while animals run from predators or build shelters. The instinct to protect oneself is a universal drive to ensure survival.

While these four activities are shared between humans and animals, there is one distinguishing factor that elevates humanity: **Dharma**. According to the *Srimad Bhagavad Gita* and Vedic philosophy, Dharma represents moral and spiritual responsibility. It's our ability to seek higher knowledge, practice self-discipline, and align our actions with righteousness. Unlike animals, humans can rise above basic instincts and pursue liberation (*moksha*) by following the path of Dharma.

A Personal Journey of Transformation

I grew up in an environment where every decision felt scrutinized, where I hesitated a hundred times before making a choice. This stifling atmosphere led me to leave the place I was born and move to a hostel. Life in the hostel wasn't easy. I relied on favors from others, a deeply humbling experience that left me feeling embarrassed and powerless. But over time, I realized these feelings were illusions created by my mind. The mind often traps us in negativity, making us dwell on our limitations rather than our potential.

When I began writing this book, I faced similar struggles. Questions flooded my mind: How should I start? What should be my first word? My first sentence? These seemingly simple thoughts were normal until they grew darker: *What if I can't write? What if I fail? What if this book isn't good enough?*

Normal Thoughts vs. Dark Thoughts

Normal Thoughts	Dark Thoughts
How should I start writing?	What if I won't be able to write at all?
What would be my first word?	What if my writing isn't good enough?
What would be my first sentence?	What if I fail completely?

Thoughts, as described in the *Srimad Bhagavad Gita*, are experiments of the mind. They can be controlled and directed. But control requires self-awareness and discipline. Here's the harsh truth: no matter how much we achieve, our ultimate destiny is death. If nothing truly belongs to us after death, then why let our thoughts imprison us? Why not master them instead?

The Steps I Took to Break Free

Overcoming the challenges posed by procrastination and self-doubt required deliberate action. Here are the three key steps I followed to reclaim control over my mind and life:

1. Do It Anyway

As an athlete, I often face moments where negative thoughts try to pull me into the comfort zone. Skipping a workout or avoiding a task feels tempting, but I follow a simple rule: *Do it anyway.* Whenever these thoughts creep in, I open my yoga mat. This small action sets the tone, and I find myself moving forward instead of giving in. The hardest part is starting, and once you begin, momentum takes over.

2. Visualization

When self-doubt strikes, I turn to visualization. Watching my highlights or clips of my idols reminds me of the path I am on. It helps me reconnect with my goals and rekindle my motivation. Visualization isn't just a mental exercise; it's a powerful tool to reinforce belief in yourself and your abilities.

3. Focus on the Ultimate Aim

Whenever I feel stuck or hesitant to take the next step, I think of my ultimate goal. This clarity helps me push past the inertia and take action. Keeping your ultimate aim in sight acts as a compass, guiding you through moments of uncertainty and doubt.

Each of these steps played a crucial role in my journey and can do the same for you. The path isn't easy, but it's worth it. Small, deliberate actions can create ripple effects, leading to transformative change. Let's explore these strategies further and equip ourselves to win at life.

The Trap of Procrastination

Many of us are familiar with the term procrastination. It's a silent thief, stealing our time, energy, and potential. Why do we let our thoughts win? Why do we delay action, knowing the consequences? Let me share a story of one of my students:

Ravi was a young footballer with dreams of making it big. He had the talent, the drive, and the skill to shine on the field. But one morning, during training, I noticed something off about him. His usual enthusiasm was missing, his passes were off, and his energy was at an all-time low.

After practice, I pulled him aside. "Ravi, is something bothering you?" I asked.

He hesitated before replying, "Coach, I don't know. It's like I've lost my rhythm. Every time I step on the field, my mind tells me I'm not good enough. It feels like I'm stuck, and no matter what I do, I can't seem to move forward."

I could see the struggle in his eyes. "Ravi," I said, "let me tell you something. Right now, your mind is like a maze—a maze filled with walls of doubt and dead ends of fear. But here's the truth about mazes: they always have a way out. The question is, are you ready to find it?"

He looked up at me, unsure. "How do I do that, Coach?"

"Start with this," I said. "Do it anyway. Show up for training, even when your mind tells you not to. When negative thoughts creep in, just step onto the field. Take the first pass. Once you're there, momentum will follow."

I paused and added, "Second, visualize your best moments. Watch your highlights, replay your goals in your mind, and remind yourself of your capability. When you feel doubt creeping in, counter it by seeing yourself succeed."

"And finally," I continued, "always keep your ultimate aim in sight. Why did you start playing football in the first place? Was it to let fear and doubt win, or was it to achieve greatness? Focus on that goal whenever you feel stuck."

Months later, Ravi stood on the pitch during the finals of a major tournament. His performance was extraordinary. He scored the winning goal and led the team to victory. As the crowd cheered, he looked at me with a smile that said it all.

In the upcoming chapter, I will delve deeper into procrastination—its causes, its effects, and most importantly, how to overcome it. I will share actionable steps to free yourself from this trap and reclaim control over your life.

This chapter is only the beginning of our journey together. Let curiosity drive you forward. Each page will bring you closer to understanding how small, deliberate changes can lead to profound transformation. Let's break free from the maze and win at life.

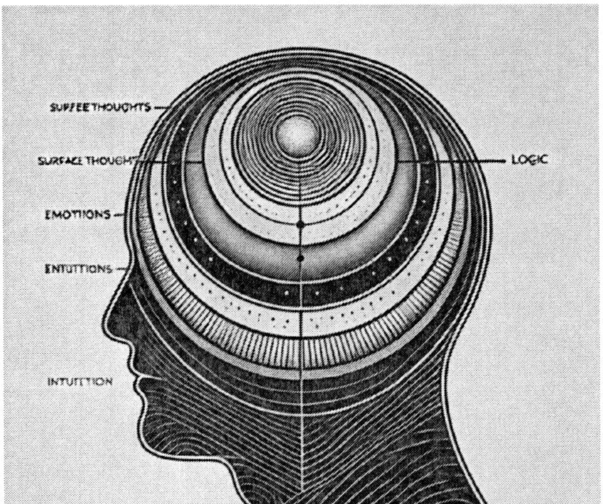
SURFEE THOUGHTS
SURFACE THOUGHT
LOGIC
EMOTIONS
ENTUTTIONS
INTUTTION

CHAPTER— 4

The Thief of Time

Delaying tomorrow, losing today

How does a person become a procrastinator? Well, I believe it stems from laziness, and this habit takes over a person's mind. When it becomes immersive, a person keeps delaying tasks for tomorrow or some other day. It's a trap, and today I'm going to tell you how to overcome it. First, let me share the definition of procrastination:

Prodespite knowing that this delay may result in negative consequences. It is not merely a crastination is the complex interplay of delaying immediate action on tasks or decisions, about putting off responsibilities but is often a manifestation of underlying psychological and emotional factors.

1. The Procrastination Paradox:

Procrastination is paradoxical in nature—it involves both an acute awareness of the tasks at hand and a simultaneous disengagement from them. This dissonance creates a cycle where the immediate comfort of avoidance outweighs the long-term benefits of completion.

2. Psychological Landscape:

At its core, procrastination is driven by a web of emotions including fear, anxiety, and self-doubt. These emotions create a barrier to starting tasks, as individuals grapple with the potential for failure or criticism.

3. Temporal Distortion:

Those who procrastinate often experience a distorted sense of time, where deadlines seem distant until they suddenly become urgent. This distortion can alter perception, making tasks appear less immediate and more manageable than they are.

4. The Role of Instant Gratification:

Procrastination often involves choosing immediate gratification over long-term rewards. Engaging in pleasurable activities as a distraction from important tasks provides a temporary sense of relief but exacerbates the cycle of delay.

5. The Emotional Toll:

Procrastination isn't just about missed deadlines; it can also lead to a persistent sense of guilt and stress. The emotional burden of procrastination can impact self-esteem and overall well-being, perpetuating a negative feedback loop.

6. Strategies for Intervention:

Overcoming procrastination involves addressing both the emotional and practical aspects of task management. Techniques such as breaking tasks into smaller, more manageable steps, setting specific goals, and employing self-compassion can help mitigate the tendency to procrastinate.

I think this helped you to know how your habit of procrastinating is killing you from the inside. Now I am sharing a few stories then I will give you a few steps and tasks as well.

A Short Story: The Fading Fire

Once, in a quaint village, there was a craftsman named Tom who prided himself on making beautiful lanterns. One day, he received a special commission to create a grand lantern for the village festival. The deadline was three months away, but Tom kept delaying the work, thinking he had plenty of time.

Weeks passed, and Tom spent his days lounging and working on minor projects, all the while telling himself he'd start the grand lantern tomorrow. As the festival approached, Tom found himself with only a week left and no progress made on the lantern.

Panicking, Tom worked around the clock. He finished the lantern just in time, but it was rushed and lacked the usual craftsmanship. At the festival, the lantern still looked beautiful, but the details and precision Tom was known for were missing.

The villagers noticed, and Tom felt a pang of regret. He realised that his procrastination had not only stressed him out but also affected the quality of his work. From that day on, Tom learned to start his projects early, ensuring he had ample time to do them justice.

Story 2: The Unwritten Letter

In a small, serene town, there lived an elderly woman named Margaret, known for her warm smile and kind heart. Margaret had a son, Tom, who lived far away. Despite their distance, they shared a special bond, and Margaret always promised herself that she would write Tom a heartfelt letter to remind him of her love and pride.

Years went by, and Margaret's promise remained unfulfilled. Each day, she thought about the letter but never found the time or energy to start. Life's daily routines and minor distractions always seemed to come first. "Tomorrow," she'd say, "I'll write it tomorrow."

One chilly autumn morning, Margaret received a call with devastating news: Tom had been in an accident and had passed away. The weight of grief was overwhelming. As she sorted through his belongings, she found a box of unsent letters—one from Tom to her, written long ago but never sent.

In the letter, Tom had poured out his love, his dreams, and his memories of their time together. Margaret's heart broke as she read his words. She realised that her procrastination had prevented her from sharing her love and appreciation when it could have mattered most.

Margaret's regret was profound. She understood now that time, once lost, cannot be reclaimed. The letter she had meant to write, filled with unspoken words and emotions, would never reach Tom. Her procrastination had deprived her of a meaningful connection with her beloved son.

In her sorrow, Margaret shared her story with the townsfolk, urging them to act on their feelings and promises before it's too late. Her message resonated deeply: "Don't wait for tomorrow to express your love and appreciation. The moments you delay may never come back."

From that day on, the townspeople carried Margaret's message in their hearts, embracing the present and cherishing their loved ones without delay.

Morals for Both Stories

1. **The Fading Fire:**
    - **Moral:** Procrastination may give temporary comfort, but it leads to regret and compromises the quality of your work. Time, once lost, cannot be regained, and rushing at the last moment can never bring your best results.

2. **The Unwritten Letter:**

   Moral: Delaying meaningful actions can result in deep regret, especially when those moments are lost forever. Life's moments and connections are precious—don't postpone the chance to express love and gratitude before it's too late.

   Procrastination can lead to deep regret, as illustrated by Tom's rushed lantern and Margaret's unwritten letter. Both characters learned too late that delaying important tasks or expressions of love can rob us of meaningful experiences and connections. ***'Procrastination is the grave in which opportunity is buried.'***

Chapter- 5

The Ripple Effect of Routine

"Small actions spark big changes."
by tizilyadav

Before I start writing about this chapter, I would like to ask yourself a question- What is 'Action' and 'Reaction'? I Hope everyone of you has listened about the third law of newton- "Every action has an equal and opposite reaction". Conversely, in our lives every action plays a reaction whether it's a tiny action or Massive action. If you are a doctor and you ask an ill patient to take pills(action), the medicine will always recover(reaction) the patient's body. Conversely, if you're a procrastinating person and tell yourself daily that I will start to go to gym tomorrow, then this is obvious to become weak.

Changes our must and this custom has been followed from ***The oldest era in Earth's history 'the Archaean era'***. Even in today's world you can find thousands of changes in your daily life and around you as well. I don't believe in magic if you snap your finger and things happen on their own. Lets say, you want to become a billionaire but you do nothing to achieve that goal, Would you ever become a billionaire? Vice-Versa you do take a tiny action daily towards your goal, even this is not a surety of becoming a billionaire but at least this ensures to take you closer to your goal. Your daily habits, no matter how small, can create a lasting impact on your life. Just like a drop of water creates ripples in a pond, a single positive routine can influence your future in unexpected ways.

I believe Change is the process of Consistency. Doing something small every day might not seem like much, but over time, it builds up. Whether it's reading a page, exercising for five minutes, or practising mindfulness, these little actions lead to big changes. For an example- you're improving 1% daily and working consistently for the one month, for the first 1 week you'll improve up to 7% only which can be neglected but after one month when you'll improve up to 30% only then you'll see the effect of the ripple. We'll discuss more about this but for now, I am sharing a story with you but before that do a small exercise. Close your eyes and think about what you wanna do for today.

Once upon a time, a saint came to a random house and asked the owner if he could get something to eat. The owner's son is a 21 years old boy named Rudraksh. The boy was noticing the process. He starts to think about the saint's life and says to his own mind, "this is so easy to survive. They don't study, nor do they have any burden on them for their career. Now the boy desperately wanted to become a saint. He asked his mom, I want to live like a saint or a monk. His mom replied, dear it is not easy to live like a monk. It asks for many sacrifices but the boy was yearning and wanted to become a saint. The boy kept thinking and planning to become a saint.Next morning the boy left his home secretly and decided to head north. His mom registered an FIR but even the cops couldn't find the boy.

After several years, the boy became a complete Monk, and he was called up for a school ceremony. The organiser asked him to give a few tips to students about how to win in life. The first thing the saint said was- "In the arena of life the winner is who doesn't think of the next move" and the second tip was- "Fabricate your own path, don't follow the trace".

The story emphasises that what may seem easy and desirable on the surface often requires immense sacrifice, dedication, and understanding. True success in life doesn't come from following the easy path, but from forging one's own way and living with mindfulness and purpose.

Perception vs. Reality:

- Rudraksh initially believed that the life of a monk was easy because it appeared to have no obligations like education or career stress.
- This highlights how we often misjudge situations by looking only at the surface, without understanding the deeper commitments involved.

Yearning for a Different Life:

- Rudraksh's desire to become a monk reflects how young minds can feel burdened by societal expectations (education, career) and yearn for a life that seems simpler or more meaningful.

Sacrifice and Commitment:

- His mother's advice that becoming a saint is not easy suggests that any meaningful path requires sacrifice. This can apply to various aspects of life, whether spiritual, personal, or professional.

Personal Growth Through Experience:

- Rudraksh's secret journey shows that sometimes personal growth requires us to step away from our comfort zones and take bold, independent steps.
- His transformation into a monk wasn't instant; it took years of dedication and living through challenges.

The Two Lessons from the Saint:

- **"The winner doesn't think of the next move"**: This suggests living in the present moment, focusing fully on each step, rather than overthinking or planning excessively for the future.
- **"Fabricate your own path, don't follow the trace"**: This is a call for individuality and courage in making life choices. It speaks to the importance of self-direction and not blindly following the crowd.

Rudraksh's journey shows that life's not about escaping challenges but about learning to face them with clarity and purpose. His final lessons teach students that success and fulfilment come from living authentically and with presence. There is no shortcut to success.

Remember, I Asked the you to close your eyes before sharing the story serves a powerful purpose. It helps to disconnect from external distractions and focus your full attention on the narrative. By doing this, you create a more immersive experience, allowing you to visualise the story and engage emotionally with Rudraksh's journey.

Additionally, closing your eyes can symbolise introspection and openness, aligning with the deeper themes of the story, such as self-discovery, mindfulness, and personal growth. It encourages you to reflect on your own perceptions and experiences, much like how Rudraksh's initial thoughts about a monk's life shifted as he gained deeper understanding. The purpose of sharing this story was to give you a brief about success. Like I said "there is no shortcut to success". Now get back to the ripple effects now I will share a few key actions which you should bring to your life-

The Power of Compounding Improvement: Just like in the example of improving 1% daily, you can emphasise how small efforts add up. After 30 days, you're not just 30% better, but the improvements build on each other, creating exponential growth. You can compare this to compound interest, where small investments grow significantly over time.

Usain Bolt, the fastest man in the world, wasn't made overnight. For years, he trained consistently, focusing on small improvements in speed, technique, and endurance. Even when results weren't immediate, he trusted the process. His legendary sprint in the 2008 Olympics, where he set world records, was the culmination of daily, incremental efforts—proof that consistency, not sudden bursts, creates greatness.

Embrace the Long-Term Vision: Success often requires a long-term vision and the patience to stick with consistent efforts, even when progress seems invisible. It's easy to get discouraged when results don't show right away, but every small action adds up, creating a ripple effect. Just like planting a seed, you may not see immediate growth, but with time and nurturing, it blossoms. The key is to stay committed to the process, because over time, those consistent efforts compound, leading to significant results that may surprise you. Patience turns small steps into big transformations.

Daily Habits as Building Blocks: Daily habits are the building blocks of our success. Think of them as the bricks that create a strong foundation for your dreams. Each small action you take—whether it's reading a few pages, practising a new skill, or exercising—contributes to a larger structure of achievement. These habits may feel insignificant initially, but over time, they accumulate and lead to remarkable change.

For example, consider the story of a writer who commits to writing just 200 words a day. At first, it may seem trivial, but after a year, that small habit translates into a novel! This illustrates how daily habits can propel you toward your goals, transforming small actions into significant accomplishments. Embrace the power of consistency and watch your aspirations flourish!

Avoiding Burnout Through Small Actions: Avoiding burnout is crucial for maintaining long-term productivity and motivation, and small actions play a key role in this process. When we take on too much at once, it can feel overwhelming, leading to exhaustion and frustration. By focusing on manageable, consistent tasks, we can sustain our energy and passion. Small actions create a sense of achievement without the pressure of major commitments.

For instance, a busy professional might set a goal to take a 5-minute break every hour to stretch or breathe deeply. This simple practice not only rejuvenates the mind but also prevents fatigue. Over time, these small breaks accumulate, enhancing overall well-being and productivity. By integrating small actions into your routine, you create a balanced approach that keeps burnout at bay while fostering growth.

Growth in Multiple Areas: Growth in multiple areas of life is a holistic approach that enhances overall well-being and fulfilment. Focusing solely on one aspect, such as career or fitness, can lead to imbalance, causing stress and dissatisfaction. By embracing small, consistent improvements across various domains—physical health, relationships, personal development, and mental well-being—you create a rich tapestry of growth that supports each area.

For example, consider a person who dedicates 10 minutes daily to exercise, spends quality time with family, and reads a chapter of a book each evening. These small, daily actions not only foster physical fitness and knowledge but also strengthen relationships. Over time, this multifaceted growth leads to a more enriched, fulfilling life, demonstrating that progress in one area positively influences others, creating a powerful synergy.

Visual Analogies: Visual analogies can significantly enhance understanding by illustrating complex ideas through relatable imagery. When discussing growth and consistency, analogies like the **iceberg** and **plant growth** effectively convey the underlying principles.

The iceberg analogy highlights how most of an iceberg's mass remains hidden beneath the surface. Similarly, the hard work and small daily actions we take often go unnoticed initially, yet they form the foundation of our eventual success. Just as only a fraction of an iceberg is visible, only a portion of our efforts may be recognized at first.

The plant growth analogy illustrates how a seed requires consistent nurturing before it breaks through the soil. It may seem like nothing is happening for weeks, but with daily care, it eventually grows into a strong plant. This represents the idea that small, consistent actions lead to significant results over time. By using these visual analogies, we can more effectively communicate the importance of consistency and patience in achieving success.

Conclusion: As we conclude our discussion on the power of consistency and small daily actions, I invite you to take on an actionable challenge. Choose one area of your life where you'd like to see improvement—be it fitness, learning, or personal development.

Starting today, commit to making a small, consistent change. This could be as simple as dedicating 10 minutes a day to reading, going for a brief walk, or practising a new skill. Document your progress over the next 30 days.

At the end of this month, reflect on the changes you've experienced. Notice how those small actions have compounded to create meaningful growth. Remember, success is not about giant leaps but about the steady, small steps we take each day. Embrace this journey and watch how it transforms your life!
Now I am giving you a structure that you should follow no matter what stay consistent to this structure.

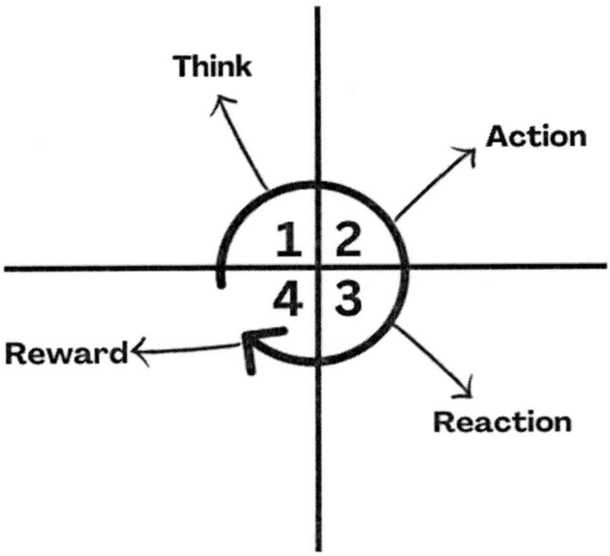

Try to observe the image. We'll discuss these life changing four steps in our next chapter.

CHAPTER- 6

From a Thought to Reward

Think, act and shape reward.

Everyone loves gifts, rewards, awards, profit, bonus, compensation, Recognition, perks. Conversely, our mind works. Our minds are naturally wired to seek rewards. Whether it's the satisfaction of completing a task or the pleasure of achieving a goal, rewards trigger positive emotions that motivate us to keep going. This is why even small wins feel so satisfying—they release dopamine, reinforcing good habits and driving us to pursue more. By setting achievable milestones and rewarding ourselves along the way, we harness this innate drive to stay focused, productive, and motivated on our path to success.

If you remember, I shared a picture in our last chapter. Think-Action-Reaction-Reward, now we'll learn about these four steps and also I'm going to give you a few tips to earn the perks of life.

Now have a look again at this picture.

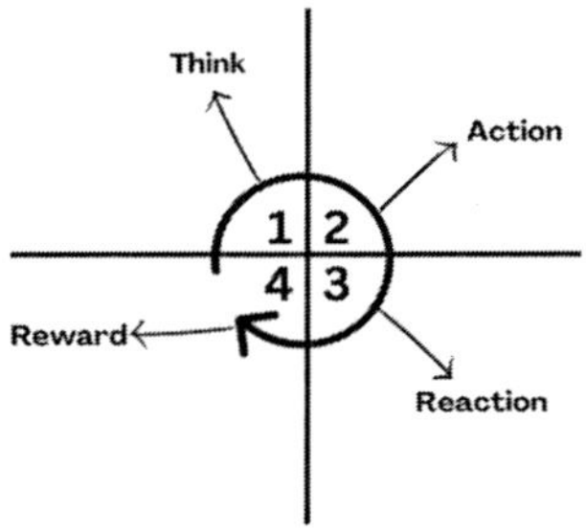

Think

This is the very first step of change. Before any action is taken, before any significant transformation can occur, it all begins with a single thought. The power of thought lies in its ability to open the door to new possibilities, allowing us to envision different realities and outcomes. It's in this crucial moment of thinking that we start questioning the status quo, reflecting on what could be different, and visualising the steps needed to create that change.

Our minds are like blueprints for action. Without thinking, there's no planning, no strategy, and no direction. The thought process allows us to identify areas in our lives where improvement is needed. It prompts us to analyse our current situation, dream of better futures, and assess the paths we can take to reach our goals. This conscious reflection acts as the catalyst for growth, pushing us out of complacency and into a mindset of progress.

However, it's important to note that thinking alone isn't enough. It is simply the seed from which change grows. But without this seed, no action can take root. Once we've formed the thought, the next steps—action, reaction, and reward—follow naturally.

In short, to initiate any change, we must first engage our minds. The act of thinking not only defines the change we wish to see but also builds the momentum necessary to turn those ideas into reality. It's the starting point, the first domino, that sets everything else into motion.

Action

It's the Bridge between Thought and Change. Action is the crucial second step in the journey of transformation, where a mere thought or idea begins to take form in reality. While thoughts and reflections are essential for identifying areas where change is needed, they are only the starting point. Action is what bridges the gap between what exists in the mind and what manifests in the world. Without action, even the most profound thoughts remain abstract, lacking the force necessary to drive change.

Once a thought has been formed, the next critical phase is to translate that thought into deliberate and consistent action. This is where the true work begins. The mind might generate countless ideas, but without execution, they remain trapped in the realm of potential. Action, therefore, is the process of turning that potential into kinetic energy—making things happen, no matter how small the first step might seem.

Taking action also requires courage and discipline. Thoughts can be safe and easy to contemplate, but stepping into action introduces real-world challenges, risks, and uncertainty. It forces us to confront the discomfort of leaving our comfort zones. However, the more we act, the more we learn adapt, and refine our approach. Action is dynamic; it allows us to adjust our course as we gain experience and insight, making it an essential part of growth.

Another important aspect of action is consistency. The transformation does not happen overnight. Small, steady steps taken daily compound over time to create significant change.

It's through repeated actions that habits are formed, and it's these habits that lead to long-term success. The power of action lies in its ability to build momentum. Even minor actions, when done consistently, generate progress and open up new possibilities.

Action also has the ability to shape not just external outcomes but also internal ones. When we take action, we reinforce our belief in our own capabilities, boosting confidence and resilience. With every step forward, we gain a clearer sense of direction, a deeper understanding of what works, and a growing sense of accomplishment. This creates a feedback loop, where the reward of seeing progress fuels further action, creating a virtuous cycle of effort and reward.

In essence, action is the lifeblood of change. While thoughts provide the blueprint, action is the construction process that brings those ideas into existence. It is the secondary but indispensable step in the journey of growth and transformation. Every great achievement, no matter how grand or complex, is built on a foundation of consistent, purposeful action.

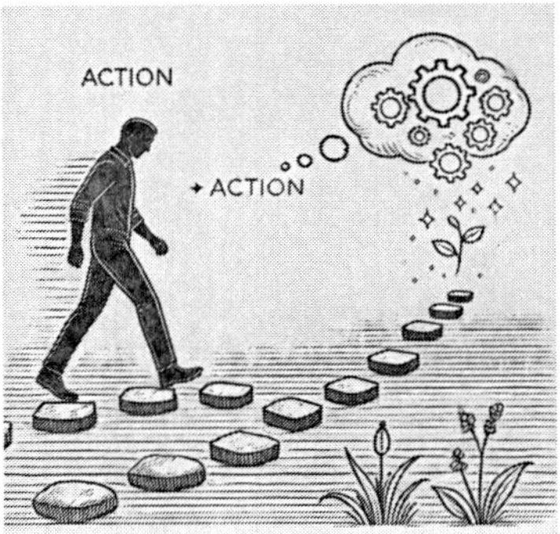

Reaction

The Crucial Third Step of Transformation. Once we've had a thought and taken action, the natural next phase is the reaction or response to the action. Reaction serves as the feedback loop in the process of transformation, helping us understand the impact of our actions and allowing us to adjust and refine our approach. Reactions can come from external sources—like the environment or other people—or internally, from our own reflections and feelings. Both types of reactions are critical in shaping the future course of our actions.

In many cases, the reaction is immediate and observable. When we take action, we can often see results right away, whether positive or negative. For example, if someone starts working out regularly, they might initially experience soreness or fatigue. These are reactions from their body, indicating that it's adjusting to new demands. Over time, the body adapts, and these initial reactions are replaced by increased strength and endurance. This feedback allows the person to adjust their workouts, perhaps pushing harder as they become stronger, or resting when necessary to avoid injury.

In other cases, the reaction is more subtle requiring reflection and deeper understanding. When pursuing long-term goals or complex projects, the reactions may not always be immediate. For example, a business owner who launches a new product might not see instant success, but through customer feedback and market reactions, they can learn what works and what doesn't. This insight helps them fine-tune their approach, leading to better results in the future.

The key to mastering this third step is to remain open and adaptive to the reactions. Often, people fear negative reactions, but these are just as valuable as positive ones. A negative reaction doesn't mean failure—it simply means the action needs adjustment or a different approach. In fact, some of the most important lessons in life come from negative reactions, as they help us learn and grow.

It's important to also consider our internal reactions. After taking action, how do we feel? Do we experience pride, relief, or excitement? Or are we anxious, frustrated, or discouraged? These emotional reactions can offer powerful insights into whether we're on the right path or if we need to make changes.

Ultimately, reaction is about learning and evolving. By paying attention to the feedback we receive from our actions, we gain the knowledge and experience necessary to refine our approach and continue moving forward.

Example

A writer who publishes their first book may not immediately receive widespread praise. However, through reviews and reader feedback, they learn how to improve their craft. The initial reactions guide them, helping them evolve into a better writer with each new project.

Reward

The final step in the transformative journey from thought to action is the reward. This stage is not merely about external recognition or accolades; it encompasses the intrinsic satisfaction and fulfilment that arise from our efforts. Our minds are hardwired to seek rewards, and this fundamental drive plays a pivotal role in sustaining motivation and reinforcing positive behaviours.

When we achieve a goal or complete a task, the sense of accomplishment serves as a powerful reward. This feeling is not just a fleeting emotion; it activates the brain's reward system, releasing chemicals like dopamine, which reinforces the behaviour that led to the success. In essence, rewards serve as positive feedback, telling our brains, "This was worthwhile; do it again." This mechanism is why setting achievable milestones along our journey is crucial. Each small success acts as a stepping stone, creating a chain reaction of motivation that propels us forward.

Rewards can take many forms. They can be tangible, such as bonuses or promotions at work, or intangible, like personal satisfaction or the joy of learning something new. For instance, someone who commits to a regular exercise routine might feel physically stronger and healthier as a reward, while also experiencing enhanced mood and energy levels. These positive feelings reinforce their commitment to continue exercising.

Additionally, rewards can also be emotional. The fulfilment of achieving a personal goal can lead to increased self-esteem and confidence. For example, an artist who completes a painting may feel a sense of pride and joy, which can encourage them to take on new projects or challenges. These emotional rewards create a sense of identity and purpose, helping individuals align their actions with their values and aspirations.

Moreover, the concept of reward extends beyond personal gratification. When we achieve our goals, we often inspire those around us. This social aspect of rewards can be incredibly powerful. When we share our successes with others, we create a supportive environment that fosters collaboration and collective growth. This communal reward can lead to stronger relationships, teamwork, and a sense of belonging, enhancing the overall experience of achievement.

It's also essential to recognize that the journey to the reward is often filled with challenges and setbacks. The path is rarely linear, and maintaining motivation during difficult times can be tough. However, it is during these challenging moments that the anticipation of the reward becomes even more critical. By focusing on the ultimate goal and visualising the reward, individuals can push through obstacles and stay committed to their actions.

Finally, reflecting on the rewards we receive can help us understand our values and priorities. Are we pursuing external rewards for the sake of recognition, or are we seeking deeper, intrinsic rewards that align with our passions and interests? This introspection allows us to recalibrate our goals and actions to ensure that our journey remains fulfilling and meaningful.

In summary, reward is the final, essential step in the cycle of transformation. It not only reinforces our behaviours and motivates us to continue but also enhances our sense of identity and connection to others. By understanding and appreciating the rewards of our efforts, we can cultivate a mindset that embraces growth, resilience, and a love for the journey itself.

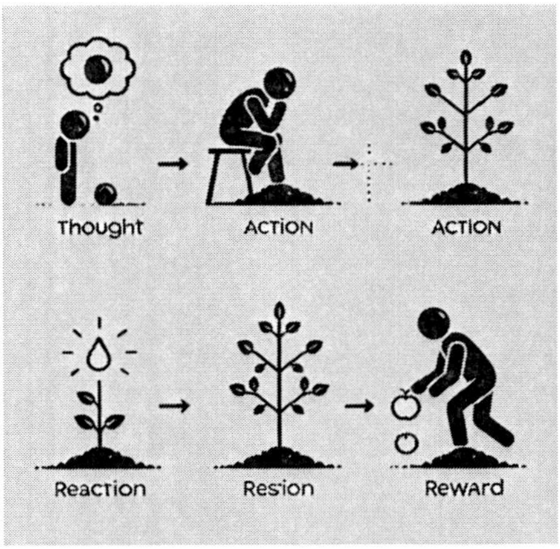

Have a look at this picture. Here is an explanation of the image. Suppose that you have thought of growing a plant in your garden- Step 1: thought. Now you have brought a few seeds of the plant and sowed the seed in the ground. Took care of the seed everyday. You give water and fertilisers as per need- Step 2: Action. Now after a few weeks the plant grows well and seems like a healthy tree- Step 3 Reaction. And the final result is you get the fruits to eat and also the shadow of the tree- Step 4: Reward.

In the example of growing a plant in your garden, the reward is essential for several reasons:

1. **Motivation and Encouragement**: The reward, in this case, the fruits and shade provided by the tree, serves as a powerful motivator. Knowing that you will eventually enjoy the fruits of your labour encourages you to invest the necessary time and effort into the initial stages of planting and nurturing the seed. This anticipation keeps you committed to the daily actions required for growth.

2. **Sense of Accomplishment**: When you see the plant flourishing and eventually bear fruit, it gives you a deep sense of achievement. This accomplishment boosts your self-esteem and reinforces your belief in your ability to nurture and grow. Recognizing your success makes you more likely to take on similar projects in the future.

3. **Reflection and Learning**: The rewards also provide valuable feedback about your efforts. If the tree bears fruit, it indicates that you took the right steps in caring for it. Conversely, if the plant doesn't thrive, it prompts reflection on what might have gone wrong. This feedback loop enhances your gardening skills and helps you make better choices in the future.

4. **Connection to Nature**: The act of enjoying the fruits and shade fosters a deeper connection to nature. It enriches your experience and makes the effort worthwhile, leading to a greater appreciation for the process of growth and the cycles of life.

5. **Community and Sharing**: Finally, the fruits of your labour can be shared with family and friends, creating moments of joy and connection. This communal aspect of rewards enhances social bonds and encourages a sense of belonging, making the entire gardening experience more enriching.

Now let me share an example of my own life. When I started to build a healthy routine, It was very hard to work with my mind. I have a bad habit of eating Noodles on a daily basis. But when I decided to leave this habit I found a few difficulties like craving,telling lies to my mind and procrastinating. So, I decided to trick my mind and give myself a few tasks- First: I told myself that I'll eat Noodles twice a week only. Then after a few weeks I decided to eat Noodles once a week only. Then I decided I will eat Noodles once a month, and today I don't feel craving for the Noodles. Similarly, I think-act-and the reaction can be seen easily. I have a healthy body with abs and obviously the reward is more tasty than the taste of the Noodles.

In summary, rewards are crucial not only for reinforcing behaviour but also for enhancing personal growth, fostering reflection, and creating connections with others. They transform the journey of growth into a fulfilling and meaningful experience.

In our upcoming chapter we'll learn about the steps of the Transformation.

The First Law-

Importance of an Attitude

Chapter- 7

Winner Mindset

'YOU'RE NOT A WINNER, THE STEPS ARE'.

"Winners don't do different things, they do things differently". If the plans come to your mind but you couldn't convert them to the action plan then I would like to share a method. **What is your ultimate goal? What steps will you take to reach it? By when do you aim to accomplish it?** When a situation like that comes to you, always think about these questions. Whenever you have to make a decision towards your goals or to bring a change in your life, apply this method.

I would like to share my love life journey. I remember it was an exam hall and I saw a girl watching on her mobile and just smiling silently. That day, at the very first sight my mind started to make dreams of me and her together. Many more thoughts were popping-up in my mind, like what if I asked her to go out and she slapped me in the front of the entire class, what if she refused to talk with me, what if she feels unsafe with my presence. Positive thoughts were also there, like if she agrees for the date maybe we can live our entire life together. I asked myself, What are my goals with her? If she says yes and the answer was simple I would like to live my entire life in her arms. So, Now the question was what steps should I take to talk with her and the answer my mind gave me, start with asking her name. Now the things were almost solved. So, I went near her and asked her for her name as I had planned. Hence, the outcome or the taste of the reward can still be tasted. Today we are living together and to be very honest I am very happy with her.

Steps to Embracing a Positive Attitude and a Winner's Mindset

1. **Set a Clear Vision**
   The first step towards a winner's mindset is to have a clear vision of what you want. Whether it's in relationships, career, or personal growth, defining your goals gives your mind a destination to work towards. In my story, you visualised what I wanted—building a life with the girl I saw. You didn't just focus on the moment but thought ahead, allowing yourself to dream of the positive possibilities. A clear vision keeps you motivated and focused, even in the face of challenges.

2. **Balance Optimism with Realism**
   A positive attitude doesn't mean ignoring the challenges or risks involved. Instead, it involves balancing optimism with realism. In my story, I acknowledged the potential negative outcomes—what if she refused, felt uncomfortable, or rejected my advances? But alongside these doubts, you allowed yourself to entertain the positive possibilities—what if she said yes, and we ended up together? This is essential for a winner's mindset: facing potential setbacks, but not letting them paralyse you. Instead, you used both the positive and negative thoughts to prepare yourself for action.

3. **Break It Down into Small, Achievable Steps**
   A key aspect of the winner's mindset is breaking down big goals into smaller, manageable steps. Rather than overwhelming yourself with the bigger goal (building

a life with her), I focused on the next immediate step—starting with asking her name. This approach keeps you from feeling daunted by the magnitude of your goals and helps you stay focused on what you can control in the present moment. Small actions compound into larger successes, and a positive mindset embraces this incremental progress.

4. **Courage to Take Action Despite Fear**
   A winner's mindset is not about the absence of fear, but about acting in spite of it. In my story, although I was aware of the risks, I chose to move forward and take the first step. This courage to act is vital for success in any aspect of life. Fear of rejection, failure, or embarrassment is natural, but a positive mindset doesn't let fear dictate your actions. Instead, it focuses on potential rewards and uses fear as a motivator rather than an obstacle.

5. **Focus on Growth and Learning**
   Each step you take, regardless of the outcome, contributes to your growth. Whether the girl had said yes or no, the mere act of taking initiative would have built your confidence and resilience. A winner's mindset embraces this growth—seeing each action as an opportunity to learn and improve, whether the result is favourable or not. This mindset ensures that you continue evolving, even when faced with setbacks.

6. **Reap the Reward of Consistency**
   The reward for consistent effort and maintaining a positive attitude isn't always immediate, but over time, the results become clear. In my story, the final reward was a loving relationship built over time, which is a reflection of my willingness to act, your consistency in pursuing the goal, and your positive attitude towards the process. A winner's mindset focuses not just on instant gratification, but on long-term rewards that come from sustained effort.

7. **Cultivate Gratitude**
   Finally, a positive attitude involves cultivating gratitude for the journey, not just the outcome. You acknowledged the happiness and fulfilment you feel from your relationship today. Similarly, in any area of life, recognizing and appreciating the small wins along the way builds positivity and reinforces a winner's mindset. It helps you stay motivated and joyful, even when things don't unfold exactly as planned.

This was just about converting a thought to a positive decision- this is the real meaning of the positive attitude. Now, I will tell you about the wrong decision and falling down again and again but still you have to stand up and fight for your dream.

Story: The Artist's Persistence

There once was a young artist named Meera who dreamed of having her paintings showcased in the country's most prestigious art gallery. She worked tirelessly, painting day and night, putting her heart and soul into her work. When she felt ready, she submitted her art for a chance to be featured.

But her paintings were rejected. The gallery owner said her work lacked the finesse and uniqueness they were looking for. Feeling dejected, Meera considered giving up. But instead of quitting, she decided to develop a "Winner's Mindset." She asked herself: *What can I improve?* *What are my weaknesses?* Then, Meera sought feedback, attended workshops, and tried new styles and techniques.

Over the next few years, Meera submitted her work multiple times, only to face rejection after rejection. But every time she was turned away, she used the criticism to refine her skills. Despite the setbacks, Meera's focus was on her growth, not the temporary failures. Eventually, after five years of relentless effort, she received an invitation from the same gallery owner, who was now amazed by her transformed work.

Meera's paintings were finally displayed, and the critics praised her as a "breakthrough artist." Through perseverance, she turned her failures into a masterpiece and achieved her dream.

Moral of the Story:

- **Rejection is Not the End, But a Beginning:** Winners don't view rejection or failure as an ultimate defeat. Instead, they treat it as feedback, a signpost guiding them toward improvement. Every "no" or setback is not an end but a new opportunity to reflect, adapt, and try again with renewed vigour. People with a winner's mindset understand that rejection is a temporary obstacle, not a permanent stop, and they use it as motivation to push even harder toward their goals.

- **Adapt, Learn, and Improve Relentlessly:** One of the defining qualities of a winner's mindset is the ability to continuously adapt and evolve. Instead of being paralyzed by criticism, winners seek it out, analysing their shortcomings to sharpen their skills. They approach failure with curiosity, asking, *What can I learn from this?* They understand that success is not just about talent, but also about perseverance, learning from every failure, and making continuous improvements.

- **Focus on Long-Term Growth, Not Immediate Results:** Winners understand that success rarely comes overnight. They keep their eyes on the bigger picture, knowing that consistent effort and gradual growth lead to lasting results. While others may be discouraged by a lack of instant rewards, those with a winner's mindset are willing to work patiently, knowing that the small steps they take today will lead to significant progress over time. They cultivate patience and trust the process, believing that persistence will eventually pay off.

- **Perseverance is the Key to Unlocking Success:** The ability to persist in the face of adversity is what ultimately separates winners from those who give up. No matter how many times they fall, winners always stand back up, stronger and wiser. They don't give in to frustration or despair but remain steadfast in their commitment to their vision. They know that each failure is simply a stepping stone toward success, and they continue forward with unwavering resolve. Perseverance is the thread that weaves together every winner's story.

A study traced to ***Harvard University*** found that when a person gets a job or a promotion, 85% of the time it is because of his **Attitude,** and only 15% of the time because of his intelligence and knowledge of specific facts and figures. It is surprising that almost every institute spends dollars to teach facts and figures, which account for only 15% of success in life.

The statistic indicating that 85% of career success is attributed to attitude, while only 15% is due to intelligence and knowledge, highlights the crucial role that personal qualities play in the workplace. This finding, often traced back to studies associated with Harvard University, emphasises that a positive attitude, strong work ethic, and effective interpersonal skills are far more important than formal education or cognitive intelligence when it comes to achieving career milestones.

In today's competitive job market, employers increasingly prioritise soft skills such as adaptability, resilience, and collaboration. These attributes often lead to better teamwork, enhanced communication, and a more productive work environment. A positive attitude can foster better relationships with colleagues and superiors, creating a supportive network that can open doors for promotions and new opportunities.

Additionally, this perspective aligns with the concept of emotional intelligence, which is the ability to understand and manage one's own emotions while also recognizing and influencing the emotions of others. Those with high emotional intelligence tend to be better leaders and collaborators, making them more valuable in any professional setting.

Ultimately, the emphasis on attitude over intelligence serves as a powerful reminder that how we approach challenges and interact with others can profoundly impact our career trajectory. In a world where technical skills and knowledge are essential, cultivating a positive and proactive attitude can set individuals apart, leading to greater success and fulfilment in their professional lives.

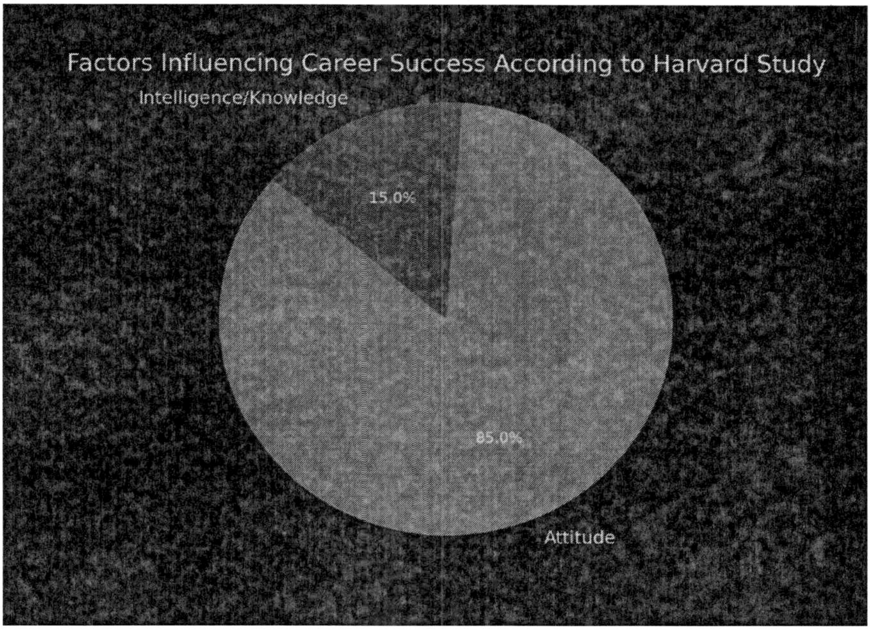

An Attitude helps you to know your potential- An attitude plays a crucial role in helping individuals recognize and harness their full potential. The way you perceive challenges, opportunities, and setbacks often determines how much effort you invest in personal and professional growth. According to a study traced to Harvard University, 85% of career success is attributed to attitude, while only 15% is based on intelligence and knowledge. This statistic emphasises the importance of a positive mindset in unlocking one's potential.

When we talk about potential, we refer to the innate abilities and talents that, when nurtured, can lead to significant achievements. However, knowing your potential is not just about recognizing skills and capabilities; it's about having the right attitude to explore them. A person with a positive attitude views challenges as opportunities to grow, rather than as obstacles. This mindset allows them to push beyond their limits, experiment with new ideas, and build resilience in the face of adversity.

Consider how attitude shapes performance in the workplace. Two employees might have similar qualifications and knowledge, but the one with a positive, proactive attitude is more likely to take initiative, seek improvement, and inspire others. This difference explains why attitude plays such a significant role in career advancement. An individual with the right attitude is not just waiting for opportunities to come their way but is actively creating them.

The power of a positive attitude lies in its ability to shift focus from limitations to possibilities. When you believe in yourself and remain optimistic even when things are tough, you unlock hidden reserves of determination and creativity. This attitude is what drives individuals to reach their full potential, as they're not afraid to take risks, learn from failure, and keep pushing forward. Those who focus only on their intelligence or past successes might shy away from risks or challenges that are crucial for growth.

A positive attitude also helps in building meaningful relationships, which are essential in personal and professional success. People are naturally drawn to those with a positive outlook, as they foster an environment of collaboration and motivation. This not only opens doors to new opportunities but also creates a support system that encourages continuous improvement.

Ultimately, attitude is the key to knowing and realising your potential. The Harvard University study shows that it is the primary factor in success, outweighing even intelligence and knowledge. When you cultivate a positive attitude, you don't just passively wait for success—you actively shape your path towards it, pushing yourself to achieve what you may never have thought possible.

Sign of Positive attitude

Here I am sharing 25 signs of the positive attitude:

Key Traits of a Positive Attitude

1. **Optimism**
    - You focus on the good in every situation.
    - *Example*: If a project fails, you look at what lessons can be learned and improve for the next one.

2. **Resilience**
    - You bounce back quickly after setbacks.
    - *Example*: After losing a competition, you train harder rather than giving up.

3. **Gratitude**
    - You appreciate the little joys in life.
    - *Example*: Feeling thankful for a friend's kind gesture, like checking in during tough times.

4. **Encouraging Others**
    - You genuinely cheer others on.
    - *Example*: Praising a colleague's presentation to boost their confidence.

5. **Smiling Often**
    - Your smile uplifts not just your mood but others'.
    - *Example*: Greeting coworkers with a smile, brightening their day.

6. **Adaptability**
    - You handle changes with grace.
    - *Example*: Adjusting quickly to a new role at work without stress.

7. **Self-Motivation**
    - You take initiative even when things get tough.
    - *Example*: Working on a personal project in your free time despite a busy schedule.

8. **Forgiveness**
    - You let go of grudges easily.
    - *Example*: Forgiving a friend who forgot your birthday instead of holding resentment.

9. **Problem Solver**
    - You focus on finding solutions rather than dwelling on problems.
    - *Example*: Fixing a flat tire and continuing your journey instead of lamenting the bad luck.

10. **Curiosity**
    - You have a thirst for learning.
    - *Example*: Reading about new technologies to stay informed.

11. **Open-Mindedness**
    - You embrace different perspectives.

- *Example*: Listening to and considering a friend's opposing political views.

12. **Complaining Less**
    - You focus on what's going right.
    - *Example*: Celebrating the small wins in a challenging project rather than venting about obstacles.

13. **Proactive**
    - You take charge of situations.
    - *Example*: Organizing a team meeting to resolve communication gaps.

14. **Good Sense of Humor**
    - You find joy in life's quirks.
    - *Example*: Laughing off a spilled coffee mishap instead of getting frustrated.

15. **Confidence**
    - You believe in yourself and your abilities.
    - *Example*: Applying for a promotion even if you're unsure of winning it.

16. **Focus on Solutions**
    - You're action-oriented in tackling challenges.
    - *Example*: Brainstorming a backup plan when a vendor cancels at the last minute.

17. **Responsibility**
    - You own up to mistakes and learn from them.
    - *Example*: Apologizing for missing a deadline and working harder to meet the next one.

18. **Supportiveness**
    - You enjoy helping others.
    - *Example*: Assisting a teammate with their workload during a busy period.

19. **Energetic**
    - Your enthusiasm motivates others.
    - *Example*: Bringing energy to team meetings, inspiring productivity.

20. **Contentment**
    - You're happy with what you have while striving for more.
    - *Example*: Finding joy in simple pleasures, like a walk in the park.

21. **Hopefulness**
    - You believe things will get better.
    - *Example*: Staying optimistic during economic downturns, believing recovery is possible.

22. **Persistence**
    - You keep going despite challenges.

- *Example*: Practicing a skill daily until you master it, no matter how long it takes.

23. **Respectfulness**
    - You treat others with kindness and empathy.
    - *Example*: Listening attentively to someone sharing a personal problem.

24. **Positive Conversations**
    - You steer discussions toward uplifting topics.
    - *Example*: Encouraging a friend to talk about their goals rather than focusing on their fears.

25. **Living in the Present**
    - You focus on the now instead of worrying excessively about the past or future.
    - *Example*: Enjoying dinner with loved ones without checking your phone.

You have almost completed a Segment of the first law. Now, tell yourself how many of you heard don't watch shorts on YT or don't watch reels on Instagram? Everyone tells you this is a waste of time, this is ruining you, this will erase your memory, this will reduce your learning capacity and so on. Well, I disagree, this will never ever create such issues if you will use it to gain Knowledge. No one knows, in today's busy lifestyle people have a lot of pressure on them, a lot of privileges. I believe that such lifestyle reels or shorts are working like a book. Like in a book we read a few pages and get a lot of the knowledge and solutions. Conversely, in the reels you scroll for a few minutes and get a lot of knowledge and day to day updates.

A positive attitude can dramatically change how we engage with content on platforms like Instagram reels or YouTube shorts. While many people might see endless scrolling as a waste of time, a person with a positive mindset approaches it with purpose and intention. Instead of mindlessly consuming whatever pops up, they seek out content that adds value to their life—whether it's learning a new skill, staying updated on current events, or finding quick solutions to everyday challenges.

With the right attitude, you can use these short videos as powerful micro-learning tools. Much like reading a chapter of a book, watching a few minutes of informative content can spark ideas, inspire actions, or even improve your mood. A positive mindset helps you filter out the noise and focus on what truly benefits you. You're able to find motivation in a quick productivity tip or learn something new in just a few seconds, turning what many consider a distraction into a tool for growth.

When you scroll with a positive attitude, you're not just consuming content passively; you're actively looking for ways to improve yourself, stay inspired, and learn something useful. It's this shift in perspective that allows you to use even the smallest moments to build yourself up, showing that positivity isn't just about what you watch—it's about how you approach what you watch.

As I named the first Law "Importance of an attitude". This is the perfect Example to understand the importance of an attitude in your life. ***"If it's in your mind,consider it done".***

Chapter- 8

Learning & Adaptation

Learning: The Foundation of Growth

Imagine a baby learning to walk. At first, they crawl, then they stand with support, and eventually, they take their first steps This process of acquiring a new skill—walking—is an example of **learning**. Learning is about gaining knowledge, skills, or behaviors through experience, observation, or study. It's a continuous process that begins at birth and lasts a lifetime, helping us grow and understand the world better.

For instance:

1. A child learning to read by sounding out letters and words. Slowly, they can recognize sentences, read books, and understand stories.
2. A person learning to cook. At first, they follow recipes, measure ingredients carefully, and gradually, they become confident enough to create their own dishes.

Learning is like adding bricks to a wall—each new piece of knowledge builds upon what you already know. Over time, this cumulative process helps you solve problems, think critically, and develop new skills.

Adaptation: The Art of Adjusting

Now let me tell you about adaptation, which is the ability to adjust when things change. Picture this: you move to a new city where people speak a different language. At first, you feel lost, but you start learning the basics of the language, observe how people interact, and slowly, you adjust to the new culture. That's **adaptation**—taking what you've learned and applying it to fit into a new or challenging situation.

For instance:

1. A student moving to a new school adapts by learning the school's rules, making new friends, and getting used to different teaching styles.
2. A plant growing in a desert adapts by developing deep roots to find water and thick leaves to store it.

Adaptation isn't just about surviving; it's about thriving. It requires flexibility and creativity, helping us make the best out of changing circumstances.

The Difference Between Learning and Adaptation

- **Learning** is like filling a toolbox with tools, while **adaptation** is using those tools to fix something.
- Learning is gradual, often driven by curiosity or a desire to grow. Adaptation is usually quicker, driven by a need to respond to changes around us.

A Real-Life Story Combining Both

When I was younger, I loved football. I practiced regularly (learning), perfecting my passes and tackles. One day, during a crucial match, the weather turned rainy, making the field slippery. I couldn't play the way I usually did, so I had to change my strategy—playing more cautiously and focusing on ground passes instead of long kicks (adaptation). Because I had practiced my skills, I could adapt quickly and help my team win.

This shows how learning and adaptation work together: what you learn prepares you to adapt when life throws challenges your way.

How People Can Benefit from Understanding Learning and Adaptation

The concepts of **learning** and **adaptation** are fundamental tools that can significantly improve personal and professional life. Here's how understanding and applying these concepts can help:

---

1. Improving Personal Growth

- **Learning** helps individuals acquire new skills and knowledge, which boosts confidence and self-worth. For example, picking up a hobby like painting or learning a new language fosters creativity and mental agility.
- **Adaptation** equips people to handle change, whether it's a shift in career, relationships, or health. By adjusting behaviors and strategies, individuals can thrive even in uncertain times.

How to Apply It:

- Set small, achievable goals for learning (like reading a chapter of a book daily).
- Practice mindfulness and flexibility to handle unexpected changes, like reorganizing plans when challenges arise.

---

2. Building Better Relationships

- **Learning** social skills such as empathy, listening, and effective communication helps people connect with others.
- **Adaptation** ensures that relationships evolve healthily, especially in the face of challenges like misunderstandings or conflicts.

How to Apply It:

- Learn to recognize and understand emotional cues in others.
- Adapt by adjusting communication styles to suit different relationships, like being more patient with a child or assertive at work.

---

3. Enhancing Professional Development

- In the workplace, **learning** helps people stay competitive by mastering new technologies, tools, and processes.
- **Adaptation** is crucial for handling workplace changes such as adopting remote work, learning new roles, or managing team dynamics.

How to Apply It:

- Continuously upskill through online courses, certifications, or mentorship programs.
- Cultivate a growth mindset to quickly adapt to organizational changes or industry trends.

---

4. Navigating Life Challenges

- **Learning** about stress management or mental health can help people understand and cope with difficulties like anxiety or loss.
- **Adaptation** ensures resilience, allowing people to recover and grow from these experiences.

How to Apply It:

- Invest time in learning mindfulness techniques, journaling, or seeking professional advice when needed.
- Embrace adaptive thinking by focusing on solutions rather than dwelling on problems.

---

5. Maximizing Opportunities

- **Learning** expands perspectives, opening up new avenues for creativity and innovation.
- **Adaptation** helps seize these opportunities by overcoming barriers or hesitations, like entering a new market or switching careers.

How to Apply It:

- Regularly explore new topics or industries outside your comfort zone.
- Adapt by experimenting with different approaches, like testing small changes before committing to a new idea.

Final Thoughts:

By recognizing the interplay between learning and adaptation, individuals can become lifelong learners and resilient problem-solvers. Whether it's mastering a new skill or navigating a major life change, these concepts empower people to grow, succeed, and thrive in an ever-changing world.

The Second Law-
Yourself

Chapter- 9

Importance of Happy Face

I often visit a café in Kamla Nagar called *MOMOS POINT*. The dining staff is exceptional, but there's one server who stands out to me—a young woman with a calm, joyful presence that seems to light up the room. Despite her worn appearance, she carries a warmth and grace that are truly admirable. I've been to this café over a hundred times, and she's served me on more than thirty occasions. Each time, her demeanour is consistent: a kind smile and a quiet resilience that puts everyone at ease.

One particular instance left a lasting impression on me. She accidentally served the wrong order to a customer who then began to yell at her, clearly frustrated and accusatory. Yet, instead of reacting defensively or becoming visibly flustered, she simply offered a soft apology with her usual smile. It was a humbling moment to witness, as she diffused the tension with such composure and empathy. Her ability to maintain such positivity, no matter the circumstance, speaks volumes. In a world where kindness is often rare, her unwavering smile has a unique power—it uplifts the atmosphere for everyone around her.

We just discussed Learning and Adaptation. So my question is- will you Adapt this habit or you'll learn from it?

I'd like to share an incident from when I was about ten years old. It was a difficult time, as my grandfather, a retired military officer who had proudly served the country for 26 years, had passed away. The entire atmosphere was heavy with sorrow; people all around were grieving, quietly reflecting on his life and the void his passing had left behind.

Among the crowd was a group of my grandfather's closest friends, all veterans themselves, who had come to pay their respects. The room was steeped in silence and sadness—until, unexpectedly, one of them looked around and, with a slight smile, asked, "So, who's up for a smoke?"

The change was immediate. Faces that had been marked with tears and solemn expressions began to shift. People exchanged surprised glances, and soon, one chuckle led to another, breaking the silence. Before long, the friends were reminiscing, sharing lighthearted stories about my grandfather, and recounting old tales of their time in the service. Laughter filled the room as they swapped memories, discussing everything from the politics of their time to humorous incidents they'd shared, almost as if they had forgotten the sadness of the day.

Watching them, I felt a rush of conflicting emotions. My grandfather's friends were laughing and joking at the very moment we were supposed to be honouring his memory. I felt anger, confusion, and a pang of disappointment, unable to understand how they could shift so quickly from mourning to laughter. But, in retrospect, I came to realise that, perhaps, this was their way of honouring him—by remembering him with joy, humour, and gratitude instead of sorrow.

A notable study on how a person's mood transitions from sadness to happiness was conducted by William James, often regarded as the father of American psychology, in the late 19th century. James proposed that emotions are not merely reactive but actively influenced by physiological changes, such as changes in breathing, posture, or even the initiation of a smile. This theory, known as the *James-Lange Theory of Emotion*, suggested that a shift in mood from sad to happy could occur simply by engaging in actions associated with happiness, such as smiling or engaging in pleasurable activities.

These two stories illustrate William James's understanding of how emotions can shift and adapt depending on circumstances, embodying his belief in the flexible, environment-influenced nature of human emotions.

In the first story at the café, the server's ability to remain calm, kind, and positive even under challenging circumstances demonstrates how our emotional responses can be influenced by choice. James's theory suggests that emotional reactions are not just automatic responses but can be guided by our behaviour. Here, the server defuses a tense situation with empathy and warmth, influencing not only her mood but also the customer's, shifting frustration into acceptance through her controlled, compassionate response. Her actions reflect James's idea that our behaviours—like smiling or remaining composed—can shape our emotions, creating a peaceful atmosphere even in the face of potential conflict. This habit of maintaining positivity under pressure could be something others adapt to handle their own challenges with resilience and kindness, showing the power of a composed emotional response.

The second story, about the gathering following the grandfather's passing, exemplifies the fluidity of emotions that James explored in his work. The veterans' shift from sorrow to laughter in the middle of mourning might seem counterintuitive, but aligns with James's insight that our emotions adapt to the immediate environment and actions. By sharing memories and humour, they created a positive atmosphere, blending joy with grief in a way that honoured the grandfather's memory. Rather than solely expressing sadness, they tapped into the full spectrum of their feelings, using humour as a coping mechanism to bring comfort to each other. This adaptive response underscores James's perspective on the power of contextual behaviours and surroundings in guiding our emotional state. Through laughter, they transformed their grief into a celebration of life, illustrating how emotional responses can adapt naturally to honour complex human experiences.

In both stories, James's theory illuminates how people consciously or unconsciously shift their emotions through behaviour and context, highlighting that our emotional lives are shaped by the balance between external situations and the choices we make in response.

Your Place

Dr. Martin Seligman, a psychologist widely known for his work in positive psychology. His groundbreaking research in the 1990s focused on how one's mindset could shape one's experience of life as either positive or negative, akin to "heaven or hell."

Seligman's **learned helplessness experiments** in the 1960s and his subsequent shift in the 1990s toward studying **learned optimism** were key in exploring this idea. In his early experiments with learned helplessness, Seligman observed that animals subjected to repeated stress without control began to act as if they were powerless to change their situation. When this behaviour was later observed in humans, it illustrated how people, too, could mentally lock themselves into patterns of negativity and despair. This foundational work revealed how one's mental state could make their experience feel overwhelmingly difficult, or even unbearable—akin to a "hell."

In the 1990s, Seligman then turned toward studying how people could train their minds to cultivate positivity, resilience, and a mindset that embraces challenges, creating what he called a "learned optimism." Through practices of gratitude, reframing challenges, and focusing on personal strengths, people could "make a heaven of hell" by changing their internal mindset. His research was one of the pioneering studies in psychology that highlighted how deeply our mental perspective can influence our experience of life's highs and lows.

"The mind is its own place, and itself can make a heaven of hell , a hell of heaven"- John Milton.

When I moved to a new place in February, I quickly realised that my small room was challenging my ability to maintain my routine. The limited space felt constraining, and I struggled to follow my usual schedule, which led to inconsistency and a sense of disorganisation in my daily activities. After a month of trying to adjust without success, I decided I needed to take immediate action to avoid further disruption.

To tackle this, I chose to divide the room into four distinct zones: a kitchen, dressing area, workspace, and study area. By compartmentalising these areas, I aimed to create boundaries within the room, assigning specific activities to each space to support a more structured lifestyle.

Kitchen Zone: I dedicated one corner to meal preparation. Setting up even a small kitchen area helped me keep cooking-related items organised, allowing me to cook more efficiently and avoid unnecessary distractions.

Dressing Area: Another section of the room was organised for dressing and getting ready. By creating this specific area, I reduced the tendency to let clothing or other items spill over into other areas, which made the room feel tidier overall.

Workspace: I set up my laptop and work-related tools on a dedicated desk, which I designated as my workspace. I made a firm rule that any work activity, like using my laptop, would only happen here. This helped to mentally compartmentalise work from other activities, which allowed me to focus better on my tasks.

Study Area: I invested in a new desk solely for studying. This separate, study-only area created a focused environment for learning. By consistently studying in this zone, I felt my concentration improve, and I was able to focus solely on my studies without interruptions from other activities.

After a few weeks of following this setup, I noticed a marked improvement in my consistency and discipline. Establishing specific zones for each part of my routine helped restore my focus and routine, which created a ripple effect on other aspects of my life. My small room had become an efficient and organised environment that supported my goals.

John Milton's quote, *"The mind is its own place, and in itself can make a heaven of hell, a hell of heaven,"* reflects the power of perspective in shaping our experiences, a principle that closely aligns with my story of transforming a cramped, unorganised room into a functional, orderly space.

Initially, moving into a small room felt restrictive, leading to frustration, inconsistency, and a feeling of chaos—almost like a "hellish" experience within my daily life. My mind was trapped in focusing on the limitations of the space, which in turn impacted my routine and discipline.

However, by reimagining the room and dividing it into distinct zones—kitchen, dressing area, workspace, and study area—I shifted my mindset. Rather than seeing the space as limiting, I began to view it as a flexible environment where each zone served a specific purpose. This mental shift allowed me to transform a potentially challenging situation into a supportive, productive space, much like turning "hell" into "heaven" through perspective. Milton's words capture this idea perfectly: the mind has the power to create positivity out of perceived limitations.

Chapter- 10

Daily Wins

Reflecting on my high school days, I remember the valuable advice my teacher shared with us: *"If you want to score better in your final exams, you should revise daily."* Back then, I didn't fully understand the significance of this guidance and never implemented it. However, after finishing school, I realised the power of consistency, and this piece of advice became one of my "favourites" for achieving long-term goals.

Over time, I've experimented with various routines to improve my lifestyle and enhance my productivity. I tried the **8+8+8 routine** (dividing the day into eight hours each for work, leisure, and sleep), the **4am routine** for an early start, and relied on **to-do lists** for daily planning. Yet, after all these trials, one routine stands out as my favourite: the **daily win** routine. This approach centres around achieving small victories every day, which prevents procrastination and builds a steady sense of accomplishment.

What makes the daily win routine so powerful is that it doesn't just help you stay on track—it actually saves time. By focusing on daily progress, I'm able to stay more productive and even free up space in my day for new tasks, interests, or relaxation. Unlike routines that can feel rigid or overwhelming, this one encourages a sustainable pace, allowing me to add meaningful goals without feeling rushed or stressed.

In the end, the routine of daily wins is more than just a method; it's a mindset that keeps me moving forward without burnout, and I truly believe it's an invaluable tool for anyone pursuing a healthier, more balanced lifestyle.

Sarah started a small online bakery called **Sweet Moments**. She dreamed of turning it into a go-to brand for gourmet desserts, but the path was challenging. As a solo entrepreneur managing everything from baking to marketing, Sarah struggled to make progress. She often felt overwhelmed by all the tasks, from creating new recipes and handling orders to promoting her business on social media.

Initially, Sarah tried following strict routines, setting ambitious goals like launching multiple new products each week and aggressively expanding her social media presence. However, this led to burnout and, worse, inconsistent results. She was spreading herself too thin, and her business was suffering from a lack of focus.

Remembering a piece of advice from a mentor—*"Small steps lead to big success"*—Sarah decided to take a different approach. Instead of aiming for huge changes all at once, she focused on what she called her **"daily win"** strategy. Each day, she set one achievable, specific goal that directly contributed to her business growth.

For example:

Day 1: Perfect one new recipe and test it with loyal customers.

Day 2: Post a high-quality photo and story about her products on Instagram.

Day 3: Reach out to two local influencers for potential collaborations.

Day 4: Review and respond to customer feedback, then make one improvement based on it.

Day 5: Research and select one local event where she could showcase her desserts.

By focusing on these small, targeted wins, Sarah was able to make steady progress without feeling overwhelmed. Over time, these daily efforts built up momentum. Her recipes improved, social media engagement increased, and customer satisfaction grew as she was consistently making improvements. She began to attract more attention, both locally and online, and her customer base steadily expanded.

After six months of following this "daily win" approach, Sarah's small bakery saw a significant boost in both reputation and revenue. Instead of constantly feeling stressed and stretched, she was moving forward with confidence, and her small daily wins were compounding into big results. Sweet Moments eventually grew into a well-known brand in her community, with loyal customers and frequent collaborations with local influencers.

A great example of a philosopher whose research aligns with the concept of daily, incremental progress is **William James**, often regarded as the father of American psychology and a significant philosopher in the pragmatist tradition. His work on habits, which he explored in the late 19th and early 20th centuries, highlighted the impact of small, consistent actions on an individual's character and achievements.

In **1890**, James published *"The Principles of Psychology,"* a monumental work in which he discussed the formation of habits and their profound role in shaping our lives. James argued that habits are formed through repeated actions and that these small, daily practices become automatic over time, influencing our behaviour and overall success. He famously said, *"Sow an act, reap a habit; sow a habit, reap a character; sow a character, reap a destiny."* This statement underscores his belief that our daily actions, when consistently repeated, create habits that ultimately shape our destiny.

James's research was one of the earliest systematic explorations of habit formation. He viewed habits as crucial building blocks for achieving long-term goals, suggesting that even small actions contribute to larger accomplishments. This philosophy has influenced a wide range of fields, from psychology and self-help to business and education, and it directly supports the idea of focusing on small, daily wins to build toward a greater goal.

Furthermore, people follow habits and I have divided them into three groups.

1. **Mimics**
2. **Conformists**
3. **Followers.**

The Mimics

Human beings are naturally inclined to mimic the behaviours they observe in their surroundings, and this innate tendency begins at birth. When a child learns to speak, their first words are often echoes of what they hear from their parents. This habit of imitating the actions and traits of those around them persists throughout life, influencing choices and behaviours in both conscious and unconscious ways.

Reflecting on my personal experiences, one moment stands out that illustrate this phenomenon. The first occurred when I was 14 years old. My father, a man of discipline and hygiene, had a unique habit: he would meticulously wash his hands before and after almost every task. At that age, I had a poor habit I'd picked up from a school friend—nail-biting. Observing my father's routine, I often found myself curious about why he was so particular about washing his hands. However, our relationship was not one of open dialogue, and I hesitated to ask him directly about his reasons. Despite this, the image of him washing his hands lingered in my mind, subtly influencing me over time.

Eventually, this silent observation led me to adopt his habit. While I didn't initially understand the rationale behind it, the repeated exposure to his action planted a seed of awareness about hygiene and cleanliness in my mind. This experience highlights how deeply the behaviours of those we look up to, even without explicit communication, can shape our habits and perspectives, underscoring the profound impact of role models in our daily lives.

Later, I found an article where I learned that it is very important for hygiene. The article was about Karachi, Pakistan's unsanitary conditions. Let me give you a summary of the article. In this article, Dr. Stephen Luby, a renowned epidemiologist, conducted research in Karachi, Pakistan, to address the public health challenges posed by unsanitary conditions. During his five-year tenure at Aga Khan University in Karachi, he focused on improving health outcomes in low-income areas. The city's poor sanitation infrastructure had led to widespread diseases, including diarrheal illnesses. His efforts included interventions to improve water quality, sanitation practices, and hygiene awareness. These initiatives highlighted the impact of systemic public health measures in reducing disease prevalence in underprivileged communities.

For more on Dr. Luby's work, you can explore resources like the Stanford University profile of his career and research contributions

Hive Digital

Existential Risks Initiative

This article inspired me to imitate my dad's habit of washing hands.

The Conformists

People often find themselves naturally aligning with the behaviours and habits of the majority around them, a phenomenon deeply rooted in human nature. This tendency stems from a desire for acceptance, belonging, and the safety of the familiar. When surrounded by a group, individuals subconsciously begin to mirror its actions, believing that the collective wisdom of many is more reliable than their own. This conformity isn't always a conscious choice—it's an instinctive response to societal cues that ensures harmony and connection. In times of uncertainty or unfamiliarity, following the majority provides reassurance and reduces the fear of standing out or making mistakes. Over time, this alignment with group behaviours shapes individual decisions and actions, often making them indistinguishable from the collective habits of their peers.

I vividly recall an incident during the COVID-19 pandemic in 2019 that exemplifies this phenomenon. At the time, fear and uncertainty were pervasive, and people adopted various practices to protect themselves from the virus. One habit that stood out to me was how people handled cash. I noticed individuals sanitising or even washing their money after withdrawing it from banks, following what seemed to be an emerging norm.

Among them was my beloved grandmother, whom I fondly call "Mummy." She had a habit of sanitising or washing cash after withdrawing her pension. Curious, I once asked her, "Mummy, why do you wash the cash every time you withdraw it? Or why do you sanitise it?" With a calm yet matter-of-fact tone, she replied, "People wash their cash too. I saw them doing this." Intrigued, I pressed further asking her what it meant. She explained, "Maybe this cash carries germs that could cause COVID. So, I wash or sanitise it to stay safe."

Her answer revealed a truth about human nature: we often imitate behaviours we observe, especially when those behaviours seem logical or protective. My grandmother wasn't alone in this practice; many around her were doing the same, driven by fear and a desire to stay safe. This incident left a lasting impression on me and inspired me to refer to this phenomenon as "the Conformist."

It's fascinating how our surroundings shape our habits, sometimes without us fully realising it. This episode from the pandemic serves as a powerful reminder of the human instinct to adapt and conform through imitation, especially in uncertain times.

The Followers

During my time sharing a room with a close friend—someone I regarded as an older brother—I came to deeply appreciate his support during my ups and downs. However, one recurring pattern of his behaviour stood out: his habit of making grand plans without ever following through. He often vowed to turn his life around, declaring his intent to jog daily, practice yoga, hit the gym, or acquire a new skill. Yet, despite his enthusiasm, his efforts would fizzle out after a few days due to a lack of consistency.

One notable aspect of his personality was his fondness for podcasts. He consumed six to seven episodes daily, drawing inspiration from motivational speakers and successful individuals. Each time he finished an episode, he would excitedly share a new strategy for achieving fitness or adopting a healthier routine. While I listened attentively and occasionally incorporated these ideas into my own schedule, I noticed he struggled to sustain these habits for more than a week. This repeated cycle made me reflect on his tendency to adopt habits from influential or famous figures but fail to maintain them.

Over time, I realised that my friend fit into a category I term as "The Follower." He sought to emulate powerful and accomplished individuals, hoping their habits would bring him success. This pattern, while well-intentioned, lacked the necessary discipline and self-awareness to turn inspiration into lasting change.

Interestingly, I've noticed this "follower" tendency in myself as well. As a devoted Liverpool FC fan, I admire Virgil van Dijk, a world-class defender. I often find myself mimicking his playing style and aspects of his disciplined lifestyle. Observing my own actions, I've come to understand why people imitate successful figures—they associate their habits with achievement and believe adopting them could bring them closer to their goals. This reflects a universal human tendency: to look up to those who inspire us and attempt to model their behaviour, even if the road to success requires more than mere imitation.

Conclusion

Human behaviour is intricately tied to the environment and the people within it. From birth, our tendency to imitate is a powerful tool that shapes our development and influences our habits throughout life. Through the examples shared, I've highlighted how this natural inclination manifests in various forms—be it mimicking the actions of those close to us, conforming to societal norms for a sense of belonging, or following the habits of influential individuals in pursuit of success.

Understanding these patterns is crucial because they remind us of how deeply interconnected we are with our surroundings and how easily habits, both good and bad, can be absorbed. While imitation can be a pathway to growth and learning, it also underscores the importance of mindfulness. By consciously choosing the behaviours we adopt and the role models we emulate, we can harness this innate tendency to build healthier, more purposeful lives. Whether as mimics, conformists, or followers, the ultimate goal is to ensure that our choices align with our values and aspirations, allowing us to grow into the best version of ourselves.

Chapter- 11

Life's Design

"What we have makes our lifestyle better, but who we have makes our lives richer". Fellow Explorers – it brings me joy to share with you that I've lived some of the best moments of my life in the past year. I've lost many friends and colleagues, but those who remain are among the most precious gifts from God.

This is a truth I've come to deeply appreciate, especially over the past year. It's a simple statement, but its meaning unfolds in profound ways when we pause and reflect.

Material possessions can make our daily routines comfortable—new gadgets, better homes, and luxurious conveniences—but these things, as wonderful as they may be, can only go so far. They cannot provide us with warmth, companionship, or the sense of belonging that people bring into our lives. At the end of the day, it is the people we share these comforts with who add depth and meaning to our experiences.

Over the past year, I've experienced some of the most memorable moments of my life, and I owe much of this joy to the people who stood by my side. I've also had to say goodbye to some friends and colleagues. The loss was heartbreaking, but it served as a reminder of how fragile and precious relationships are. Life constantly teaches us this one simple truth: we don't have forever. The people we care about today may not be with us tomorrow, so it's essential to cherish them while we can.

Think about the moments that have left the biggest impact on you. Was it buying something new or celebrating a milestone with loved ones? Was it a quiet conversation with a friend during a difficult time? These are the moments we remember, not because of what we had but because of who we were with.

Relationships require care and effort, much like tending to a garden. You need to water them, give them sunlight, and remove the weeds that might harm them. The same is true for the bonds we share with others. A simple act of kindness, a word of encouragement, or even a genuine smile can strengthen a connection in ways you can't imagine.

One of my favourite lessons from the past year is that the richness of life isn't measured by wealth or possessions but by the quality of our relationships. Imagine climbing to the top of a mountain to see the most beautiful view. If you're alone, the experience feels incomplete. But if you share that view with someone close to your heart, it becomes a memory you cherish forever.

I've realised how important it is to express gratitude to the people who matter most. Tell them you appreciate them. Say the words "thank you" and "I love you" often. These simple gestures can create ripple effects of love and positivity.

Another profound lesson I've learned is that relationships aren't always about quantity but quality. You don't need hundreds of people around you; a few good friends or family members who truly care for you are enough to make life fulfilling. A genuine connection with just one person can outweigh superficial relationships with many.

As we move forward, let's prioritise our people. Let's make time for the ones who uplift us, who stand by us during our struggles, and who celebrate our successes as if they were their own. Let's also remember to give back to these relationships, to invest time, care, and effort into nurturing them.

To my fellow explorers, my message is this: in life, we are all on a journey. The road may be unpredictable, and challenges will come and go. But with the right people by our side, we can find strength in the toughest times and joy in the simplest moments. Surround yourself with people who inspire and support you, and be that person for someone else. This is how we create a life of richness and meaning, not just for ourselves but for those around us.

In the end, the question isn't about what we accumulate but about the relationships we build. Who have you chosen to walk this journey with? Are you giving them the love and appreciation they deserve? If not, there's no better time than now to start. Let's make our lives not just better but richer by valuing the people who make it all worthwhile.

Have you ever asked yourself why people leave us, especially in our darkest moments? Are those who walk away betraying us, or is there a deeper, unavoidable process at play? Through my journey, I have come to understand that this phenomenon is neither about right nor wrong, nor entirely within human control. Instead, it is part of the natural flow of life, where every relationship, every moment, is tied to a specific time and purpose dictated by destiny.

When I started college, I had a girlfriend who was everything I could have asked for at the time. She was from a Christian family, and we shared countless joyful experiences—exploring cafés, going on trips, and simply being together. Life felt perfect, and our bond seemed unbreakable. However, as life unfolded, we found ourselves in a long-distance relationship. Despite our efforts to sustain it, the strain grew too heavy.

One day, she sat me down and said, "I think God wants us to separate. We had a good time, and I hope you understand this someday. Goodbye." Her words felt like a dagger, sudden and irreversible. For months, I was consumed by sadness and confusion, unable to process the abrupt end of what once felt eternal. My mental health took a hit, and I couldn't help but question: *Why do people leave?*

In search of answers, I embarked on a journey—both outward and inward. During one of these travels, I visited the Neem Karoli Baba temple in Uttarakhand. On the way, a saint sat beside me on the bus and struck up a conversation. Though I was in a reserved state of mind, his presence felt oddly comforting, and I found myself responding to his questions.

At one point, I asked him, "Baba, why do people leave us?" He paused and then asked me a peculiar question: "Have you ever played with a small rock while walking on the street?" I nodded, recalling countless times I had casually kicked stones during idle walks. He continued, "Why do you leave the stone after kicking it away?"

I was speechless. I had no answer to give. He smiled knowingly and said, "If you don't have the answer, find it first. Once you understand why you leave the stone, you'll find the answer to your question about people leaving."

The rest of the trip was a blur as I mulled over his cryptic words. A week later, I deliberately kicked a stone while walking. This time, I paid close attention. After a while, the stone veered off into the mud, and I realised I couldn't kick it anymore—it would dirty my shoes or cause discomfort. At that moment, the saint's question made sense.

People leave not because they choose to, but because circumstances, time, or life itself dictate their departure. Just as I stopped kicking the stone to avoid the mud, life sometimes separates us from people who might cause us harm in the long run. It's not about blame or betrayal—it's about life steering us toward what is best for our journey.

Looking back, I now understand why my ex-girlfriend said what she did. Perhaps staying together would have hindered our growth or led to unhappiness. Her parting words, though painful, were a reflection of her acceptance of life's natural flow.

This experience taught me that separation isn't inherently negative. It's often a necessary chapter in our personal evolution, helping us learn, grow, and prepare for the relationships and opportunities that lie ahead. Life's design ensures that everything and everyone comes to us at the right time and departs when their purpose is fulfilled.

So, if you ever find yourself mourning someone who has left, remember this: their exit was part of a greater plan. Trust that life knows what it's doing, even if it doesn't make sense at the moment. And instead of clinging to what's gone, focus on what remains and the new possibilities ahead.

In today's world, I've noticed a growing tendency among people to rush toward outcomes without putting in the necessary effort or embracing the process. Many individuals seem broken, lacking the courage and resilience to push past their limits. This behavior is common, especially among the younger generation, who are impatient for results and often abandon their goals when faced with challenges.

Let me share a personal experience from 2021 when I was determined to achieve six-pack abs. I followed a simple yet effective formula: focusing on consistent effort without obsessing over the immediate results. My routine was straightforward: every day, I worked out diligently and recorded my progress in a journal. Writing down my accomplishments at the end of the day gave me a sense of achievement and motivation to push harder the next morning. A quote I came across during this time became my mantra: *"Being consistent may not guarantee success, but a lack of consistency will guarantee failure."*

One day, a close friend approached me, seeking help to lose weight. I agreed to help, and we decided to join the same gym. We both paid for two months of membership, but while I attended regularly, he came only about 20 times out of 60 days. Eventually, he expressed frustration about gaining two kilograms instead of losing weight. I pointed out the obvious: *how could he expect results when he wasn't putting in the work?*

Despite his good intentions, my friend struggled because of:

1. **Excuses**: He repeatedly justified his absence with excuses like emergencies, work commitments, or social engagements.

2. **Lack of Discipline**: He couldn't stick to a routine or prioritize his goals.

3. **Distractions**: He gave more importance to temporary pleasures and external factors than to his health.

4. **Focus**: His attention wavered, preventing him from maintaining a consistent effort.

This isn't just his story—it's a reflection of many people's struggles. The root cause lies in an inability to manage oneself effectively. To overcome this, I suggest following the principle of **Run, Record, Revise**:

1. Run: Taking the First Step and Maintaining Momentum

"Run" signifies action—the cornerstone of all achievements. Without taking the first step, even the most well-laid plans remain dreams. Running doesn't necessarily mean physical activity; it symbolizes putting effort into whatever goal you're pursuing, be it health, academics, a career, or a personal passion.

Many people fall into the trap of overthinking and planning excessively, often paralyzing themselves with doubts and fears. The mantra here is simple: *Start now, improve later.* You don't need perfect conditions or extensive preparation to begin; you need determination. Starting small—whether it's a 10-minute walk, a single-page journal entry, or a single task off your to-do list—helps build the momentum necessary to sustain long-term habits.

Once you begin, consistency becomes the key. Running daily, metaphorically or literally, teaches discipline. For example, if you're working on fitness, committing to regular exercise instills a sense of responsibility toward your health. The act of showing up, even on bad days, reinforces your dedication.

2. Record: Tracking Progress for Accountability

The act of recording creates structure and accountability in your journey. Keeping a journal, maintaining a logbook, or using apps to track progress ensures you have a tangible record of your efforts. When you see your actions reflected in data—whether it's calories burned, pages read, or goals achieved—it acts as positive reinforcement.

Moreover, recording progress provides clarity. For instance, in fitness, keeping track of workouts and diets helps identify patterns and areas that need improvement. If your goal is to build a skill, recording daily practice hours reveals whether you're putting in enough time or need to adjust your efforts.

Recording isn't just about numbers—it's a tool for self-awareness. By jotting down not just your accomplishments but also your struggles and thoughts, you create a comprehensive map of your journey. This map serves as motivation when you feel stuck, reminding you how far you've come.

3. Revise: Reflecting and Improving

The final step is *Revise*—the process of reflecting on your journey and making necessary adjustments. Not everything will work perfectly from the start. Revising allows you to identify what's effective and what isn't, ensuring you don't waste time on strategies that yield little progress.

For example, in your gym routine, you may notice through recording that certain exercises aren't delivering the results you want. Revising might involve consulting a trainer, researching new techniques, or even tweaking your schedule to fit your energy levels. Similarly, in academic pursuits, revision could mean exploring different study methods or balancing subjects more effectively.

Reflection also helps you reconnect with your "why." When you revise, you revisit your initial goals and assess whether they still align with your current aspirations. This prevents burnout and keeps your purpose fresh in your mind.

Integrating Run, Record, Revise Into Daily Life

- **For Fitness**: Commit to daily exercise (*Run*), track your progress using a fitness app or journal (*Record*), and periodically review your routine for effectiveness (*Revise*).

- **For Career Goals**: Work on tasks that align with your aspirations (*Run*), maintain a to-do list or project tracker (*Record*), and evaluate your progress during weekly reviews (*Revise*).

- **For Personal Growth**: Dedicate time to self-improvement activities like reading or meditating (*Run*), write about your experiences in a journal (*Record*), and periodically reassess your habits and goals (*Revise*).

By adopting "Run, Record, Revise," you create a sustainable framework for progress. It's not just about reaching the finish line—it's about growing stronger, wiser, and more resilient along the way.

The Third Law-
Enlightenment

Chapter-12
The Five W's

In this chapter, I present to you the five W's—**Workout, Worship, Work, Write, and Wisdom**—a framework designed to guide individuals toward a life of balance, growth, and fulfillment. These five pillars have played a transformative role in my personal development, enabling me to thrive physically, mentally, and spiritually.

Today's world is chaotic; people often struggle to manage their time effectively or create structured routines. True success in life, I believe, comes from achieving a **Physical Win, Mental Win, and Spiritual Win**—a synergy made possible by integrating the five W's into daily life. Let's begin with **Workout**, the cornerstone of physical well-being.

Workout: Building a Foundation for Physical and Mental Clarity

Scientific research has long validated the importance of regular exercise for maintaining optimal health. A groundbreaking study funded by the National Institutes of Health (NIH) demonstrated how physical activity positively influences cellular and molecular mechanisms in the body. Regular workouts enhance immune function, optimize metabolic processes, and reduce inflammation, ultimately reducing the risk of chronic illnesses such as cardiovascular diseases and diabetes. Furthermore, exercise promotes the release of endorphins, chemicals that improve mood and combat stress, fostering both mental and emotional resilience.

My Journey with Workout

I began my fitness journey as a teenager, waking up early to exercise with a close friend. Our sessions were competitive but fun; we challenged each other with planks and wall-sits, each trying to outlast the other. While he consistently beat me at wall-sits, I was unbeatable in the plank challenge. At the time, we lacked a deep understanding of the scientific benefits of exercise. For us, it was all about getting six-pack abs and impressing our peers.

During summer breaks, we doubled our efforts, working out twice a day. These early experiences laid the foundation for my current fitness routine, even though life eventually took my workout partner to a hostel. As I transitioned to working out alone, I realized that the discipline and endurance we built back then continue to benefit me today.

The Payoff of Consistency

The consistent practice of those planks, pushups, and wall-sits has paid dividends. Today, my body reflects the hard work of my youth, a reminder that "**Hard work**

always pays off." More importantly, exercise has become a tool for mental clarity and decision-making. Each session clears my mind, allowing me to approach challenges with focus and determination.

Why Workout Matters

Workout is more than physical exertion; it's a path to understanding your own limits and surpassing them. It teaches discipline, fosters resilience, and reveals your true potential. Each pushup or sprint is a step toward becoming the best version of yourself, and the benefits extend far beyond the gym or the park.

Extended Insights: Workout and Holistic Health

Research highlights the holistic impact of exercise. A study published in the journal *Psychological Bulletin* found that regular physical activity improves cognitive functions like memory and problem-solving skills. It also acts as a natural antidepressant, alleviating symptoms of anxiety and depression. Additionally, strength training enhances bone density and muscle health, critical for long-term vitality, especially as we age.

The American Heart Association recommends at least 150 minutes of moderate aerobic activity weekly to maintain cardiovascular health. Pairing this with strength training ensures a comprehensive fitness regime that supports both physical and mental health.

Final Thoughts on Workout

Workout is not just about physical aesthetics; it is about cultivating a lifestyle of discipline, endurance, and self-care. Whether you're running, lifting weights, or simply walking, every step counts toward a healthier, happier you.

Incorporate workout into your routine, and you'll not only achieve a Physical Win but also unlock the mental and spiritual clarity needed to excel in other areas of life. The journey is challenging but deeply rewarding—just take that first step, and the rest will follow.

Worship: A Pathway to Inner Peace

Inner peace is a universal pursuit, yet achieving it often feels elusive. For over sixteen years, I wandered in search of tranquility. Many advised me to seek saints or delve into holy texts, but these paths, though enlightening, did not provide the inner calm I sought. Eventually, through reflection and experimentation, I discovered a set of practices that brought me closer to the state of inner peace. Among these, Worship holds a profound place, supported by complementary activities like Meditation, Chanting, Yoga, and even creative outlets like Drawing.

Here is an organized exploration of these practices and their impact:

Meditation: The Foundation of Inner Stillness

Meditation is more than a spiritual exercise; it is a scientifically proven method for achieving inner calm and mental clarity. Studies published in journals like *JAMA Psychiatry* show that regular meditation reduces symptoms of anxiety and depression by promoting mindfulness and emotional regulation. It allows individuals to disconnect from the noise of the outside world and focus on their inner being.

For me, meditation became the cornerstone of my journey toward inner peace. Setting aside even ten minutes daily to sit in stillness helped me realign my thoughts, declutter my mind, and embrace a sense of presence.

How to Practice Meditation for Inner Peace

- Start Small: Begin with 5–10 minutes a day.
- Find a Quiet Space: Choose a place free of distractions.
- Focus on Breathing: Deep, rhythmic breathing centers the mind.
- Be Consistent: Regular practice amplifies benefits over time.

Chanting: Vibrations of Peace

Chanting is another powerful tool for achieving serenity. Rooted in ancient traditions, chanting uses rhythmic sounds to create vibrations that calm the mind and elevate the spirit. Research from *Frontiers in Psychology* highlights how chanting reduces stress hormones like cortisol, fostering a state of relaxation.

When I began incorporating chants into my daily routine, I noticed a profound shift. The repetition of mantras, especially those with deep personal or spiritual significance, helped me feel more connected to myself and the universe.

Tips for Effective Chanting

1. Choose a mantra that resonates with your beliefs or goals (e.g., "Om Shanti" for peace).
2. Focus on pronunciation and rhythm for maximum effect.
3. Chant with intention—visualize the peace or outcome you seek.

Yoga: Harmony of Body and Mind

Yoga bridges the physical and spiritual realms, creating a synergy that fosters inner peace. Regular yoga practice improves flexibility, strength, and balance while promoting mindfulness and reducing stress. A landmark study published in *The Journal of Alternative and Complementary Medicine* found that yoga enhances parasympathetic nervous system activity, leading to reduced stress and improved emotional well-being.

In my personal journey, yoga became a physical embodiment of peace. From the flowing movements of Surya Namaskar (Sun Salutations) to the stillness of Savasana (Corpse Pose), each posture brought me closer to understanding my body and mind.

Drawing: Art as a Meditative Practice

Creativity can be an unexpected but effective pathway to peace. Drawing, sketching, or even simple doodling engages the mind in a focused and relaxing activity. Studies from the *American Art Therapy Association* suggest that art therapy alleviates stress, promotes mindfulness, and enhances self-expression.

For me, drawing became a unique form of meditation. Whether it was shading a landscape or creating abstract patterns, the act of putting pencil to paper silenced my thoughts and allowed me to immerse myself in the present moment.

Worship: Connecting with the Divine

Worship is a deeply personal and spiritual practice, offering a way to connect with something greater than oneself. Whether through prayer, rituals, or simply moments of gratitude, worship fosters humility, reflection, and inner calm.

Incorporating worship into my daily routine brought me a profound sense of purpose. Each act of devotion—whether lighting a candle, reciting prayers, or simply expressing gratitude—felt like a conversation with the universe, aligning my mind and spirit with higher energies.

Creating Your Inner Peace Framework

If you're seeking inner peace, consider integrating these practices into your routine:

1. Meditation: Start your day with silence and mindfulness.
2. Chanting: Use mantras to uplift your spirit.
3. Yoga: Move your body to harmonize with your mind.
4. Drawing: Explore creativity as a meditative process.
5. Worship: Foster a spiritual connection through devotion or gratitude.

Each of these practices is like a piece of a puzzle, coming together to create a life of balance and tranquility. The journey may not always be straightforward, but with consistent effort, inner peace is within reach.

Embrace these steps, and watch as your life transforms into a harmonious blend of calm, clarity, and purpose.

Work: The Art of Turning Thought into Action

Work is not just a means to survive; it is a dynamic process that transforms potential into performance. It is the art of consistently applying effort to create something meaningful, to solve problems, and to contribute value. For many, work is deeply personal, with its meaning evolving based on individual perspectives and life circumstances.

When thoughts are turned into actions, they manifest as work. This journey—from idea to execution—is the essence of growth, success, and fulfillment. To understand the diversity of work's impact, I have divided it into several lenses through which people perceive it:

Work as Chaos

For some, work is chaotic, a whirlwind of tasks, deadlines, and endless responsibilities. It often feels overwhelming and unmanageable. This perspective is common in people juggling multiple roles or those in high-pressure environments where clarity is scarce.

However, chaos at work can also serve as a catalyst for growth. Learning to navigate through disorganization helps in building resilience, problem-solving skills, and the ability to prioritize effectively.

Work as Ethics

For others, work is an embodiment of ethics—a commitment to doing the right thing with integrity and diligence. People who view work this way often find pride and satisfaction in maintaining high standards.

Ethical work fosters trust and credibility, both personally and professionally. It encourages individuals to take ownership of their actions and build legacies rooted in respect and reliability.

Work as a Burden

Sadly, for some, work feels like a burden—a weight that drags them down. This is often the case when individuals lack passion for their tasks, feel undervalued, or are unable to see the bigger purpose behind their efforts.

To transform this view, it's essential to reframe work as an opportunity rather than an obligation. Finding meaning in even the smallest tasks can shift perspectives and spark motivation.

Work as Legacy

For a few, work is synonymous with legacy. These individuals approach their efforts with a sense of purpose, striving to leave a lasting impact. Whether it's creating something innovative, mentoring others, or contributing to a cause, their work reflects their values and aspirations.

Legacy-driven work inspires not only the individual but also those around them. It turns ordinary tasks into meaningful contributions that resonate beyond one's lifetime.

Work as Identity (Dressing)

For some, work is like dressing—it reflects their identity, creativity, and individuality. These individuals pour their personality into what they do, treating their work as an extension of themselves.

This perspective is common in fields like art, design, or entrepreneurship, where self-expression plays a significant role. Even in other professions, adding a personal touch to one's work can make it more fulfilling and rewarding.

Work as Life's Essential Pillar

For many, work is simply a way to sustain life. It provides the resources needed for survival and supports their families. While this view may lack the passion or deeper connection others find, it remains a vital part of life.

Steps to Redefine Work

1. **Align Work with Values**
   Understand what you value most in life and find ways to integrate these principles into your work. Whether it's creativity, service, or innovation, aligning work with values increases satisfaction.

2. **Focus on Progress, Not Perfection**
   Work doesn't have to be flawless; it just needs to move forward. Celebrate small

wins and recognize the impact of incremental progress.

3. **Create Purpose in Tasks**
   Even repetitive or mundane tasks can be meaningful when viewed as stepping stones toward larger goals. Look at the bigger picture to find motivation.

4. **Build Strong Work Ethics**
   Approach every task with integrity and responsibility. Ethical work creates trust, satisfaction, and long-term rewards.

5. **Balance Work and Life**
   While work is essential, balance is equally important. Avoid burnout by setting boundaries and making time for personal growth, relaxation, and relationships.

Work as Growth

Ultimately, work is not static; it evolves as we do. Whether chaotic or structured, a burden or a legacy, work is what we make of it. By understanding its diverse roles in our lives and learning to approach it with purpose and perspective, we can transform it into a powerful tool for personal and professional growth.

Through dedication, reflection, and effort, work becomes more than an obligation—it becomes an art form, a legacy, and a path to fulfillment.

Writing: The Transformative Power

Writing is one of the most profound tools for personal development, communication, and emotional well-being. For me, writing is not just a skill I learned but a transformative journey that reshaped my life and mindset. Surprisingly, this journey didn't start out of love for writing—in fact, it began with reluctance and resistance.

The Reluctance of Childhood

As a child, writing was the last thing I enjoyed. I dreaded my teacher's holiday homework assignments, which were often focused on improving handwriting. The exercises felt monotonous, and I found ways to avoid them—usually by enlisting the help of my elder sister to complete them. My mother, understandably frustrated, would scold me, urging me to take the task seriously.

At that age, I couldn't grasp the purpose behind the effort. I failed to see how practicing handwriting or completing those exercises could benefit me in the long run. For me, writing was just a chore—a box to tick off during summer breaks.

The Realization in Upper Primary

Things changed when I was promoted to upper primary school. It was then that I began to understand the broader purpose of those dreaded writing assignments. They weren't just about penmanship; they were about building foundational skills:

- **Speed and Efficiency**: Regular writing practice helped improve not only my handwriting but also my speed—a crucial skill for taking notes and completing exams.
- **Depth of Understanding**: Writing required me to engage more deeply with the topics, fostering critical thinking and comprehension.
- **Expression and Creativity**: Writing became a medium to organize my thoughts, tell stories, and explore ideas.

I realized that the tasks I once disliked were carefully designed to help me grow—not just as a student, but as an individual capable of expressing and articulating ideas.

Writing as a Tool for Mental Well-being

As I grew older, writing became much more than an academic exercise. It evolved into a powerful tool for emotional regulation and mental clarity. Today, when people ask me how to manage overthinking or anxiety, my first advice is simple: *write about it.*

Journaling, in particular, is an incredibly effective practice. Writing down your thoughts, fears, or experiences helps externalize them, making them less overwhelming. It creates space between you and your emotions, allowing you to reflect and find clarity.

Research has also highlighted the benefits of journaling:

- **Stress Reduction**: Studies show that expressive writing can reduce stress and improve mental health by helping people process emotions.
- **Problem-Solving**: Writing forces the brain to organize thoughts, making it easier to identify solutions.
- **Self-Awareness**: Journaling fosters introspection, helping individuals understand their triggers, patterns, and personal growth over time.

Our minds already hold the answers to many of our problems. Writing is a way to unlock those answers, revealing insights that might remain hidden amidst the chaos of thoughts.

The Art of Journaling

If you're new to journaling, here are some steps to get started:

1. **Set a Routine**: Dedicate 5-10 minutes daily to journaling, either in the morning to set intentions or at night to reflect on the day.
2. **Write Freely**: Don't worry about grammar, spelling, or structure. Write as if you're talking to yourself.
3. **Ask Questions**: Reflect on prompts like *What am I grateful for today?* or *What's bothering me right now?*
4. **Be Honest**: Authenticity is key. Your journal is a safe space, so express yourself freely.

Writing as a Lifelong Practice

Today, writing has become one of the most cherished parts of my life. It's no longer about perfect penmanship or completing assignments; it's about growth, connection, and expression.

Whether it's journaling to process emotions, planning for the future, or creating something new, writing is a skill that continues to enrich my life. Looking back, I'm grateful for those summer assignments and my mother's persistence—they laid the foundation for a practice that has become my sanctuary.

So, if you're looking for clarity, peace, or simply a way to connect with yourself, pick up a pen and start writing. You might just discover the answers you've been searching for.

Wisdom:

The Role of Wisdom in Manifestation and Transformation

When it comes to turning dreams into reality, wisdom is the bridge between thoughts and actions. Many motivational speakers emphasize the power of manifestation but often fail to delve into how it truly works. Manifestation, as transformative as it is, requires more than just wishful thinking; it demands wisdom. Wisdom enables us to harness our energy, focus on our goals, and take strategic steps toward achieving them.

What is Wisdom?

At its core, wisdom is the ability to make sound decisions by combining knowledge, experience, and good judgment. It involves more than intellectual understanding—it's about applying insights practically and purposefully. Wisdom is the compass that guides us to act wisely, think critically, and work effectively. It is the essence of what many refer to when they say, "Work smart, not just hard."

The Role of Wisdom in Manifestation

Manifestation is often misunderstood as simply wishing for something and waiting for it to materialize. In reality, it's a structured process involving:

1. **Clarity of Desire**: Knowing exactly what you want.
2. **Focused Intention**: Directing energy and thought toward that goal.
3. **Action**: Taking consistent steps to make the vision a reality.

Wisdom is the element that ensures each step is deliberate and aligned with the desired outcome. It helps avoid impulsive decisions, distractions, and unnecessary detours.

For example, imagine someone who wants to start a business. Manifesting this vision isn't about sitting idly and dreaming—it's about acquiring knowledge, creating a plan, building skills, and executing the idea with persistence and adaptability. Wisdom plays a key role in recognizing when to pivot, how to allocate resources, and how to navigate challenges.

Why Wisdom Matters During Low Points

In life's lowest moments, wisdom becomes a lifeline. It provides the perspective needed to turn adversity into opportunity. When everything feels uncertain, wisdom allows us to:

- **Pause and Reflect**: Assess what's within our control and what's not.
- **Reframe Challenges**: See setbacks as lessons rather than failures.
- **Make Informed Decisions**: Choose the path forward based on logic and intuition rather than fear or impulse.

For instance, during times of failure, wisdom prevents us from making rash decisions. Instead, it encourages us to learn from the experience, adjust our approach, and try again with renewed understanding.

Wisdom in Daily Life

Wisdom isn't a one-time effort; it's a practice that influences every aspect of life. Here are ways to cultivate wisdom:

1. **Self-Awareness**: Understanding your strengths, weaknesses, and values.

2. **Lifelong Learning**: Staying curious and open to new ideas.
3. **Mindfulness**: Being present and thoughtful in your actions.
4. **Seeking Advice**: Learning from others' experiences.
5. **Reflection**: Taking time to analyze your decisions and their outcomes.

How Manifestation and Wisdom Transformed My Life

I've experienced the power of wisdom in my own journey of manifestation. When I was at my lowest, unsure of my next steps, I turned inward to reflect. I focused on what I wanted, wrote it down, and mapped out a strategy. Wisdom guided me to identify the resources I had and prioritize my efforts.

This process taught me that success isn't just about working harder—it's about working smarter. It's about making decisions that align with your values and purpose.

A Thought to Carry Forward

Manifestation works when paired with wisdom. It's not just about visualizing success; it's about taking informed, intentional actions that move you closer to your dreams. Wisdom is the silent force that keeps us grounded, focused, and resilient.

As you embark on your own journey, remember: Every action should stem from a place of insight and understanding. With wisdom as your guide, you can transform any thought into reality.

Chapter- 13

Grudges are negotiable

Introduction
Grudges, like any other emotional baggage, weigh heavily on the mind and spirit. Yet, when closely examined, most grudges stem from misunderstandings, minor incidents, or unchecked emotions that can often be resolved or ignored. I, too, once held onto grudges and blamed others for my unhappiness, until I learned the value of perspective. This chapter explores how grudges arise, how adopting a broader perspective can neutralize them, and why forgiveness is an essential skill for personal growth.

Personal Reflection: My Journey with Grudges

When I was sixteen, I harbored resentment toward my aunt, convinced that she was the root cause of family conflicts. At the time, I failed to see the bigger picture—that every argument involved multiple factors and individuals. As I grew older, I learned a vital truth: *It takes two to tango.* No disagreement or conflict occurs in isolation.

This realization became the foundation for my journey toward letting go of grudges. I began to question my assumptions, challenge my emotional responses, and adopt what I now call the *Wider Perspective.*

The Power of Perspective

1. The Smaller Perspective
When we adopt a smaller perspective, we focus narrowly on an incident or individual without considering the broader context. This limited viewpoint often magnifies the issue, fueling resentment and emotional distress.

For example, if someone criticizes you, the smaller perspective might interpret it as a personal attack, leading to anger or defensiveness.

2. The Wider Perspective
In contrast, the wider perspective encourages us to look beyond the immediate incident. It involves asking reflective questions, such as:

- Why did this happen?
- What role did I play in this situation?
- What are the potential consequences of holding onto this grudge?

Adopting a wider perspective shifts the focus from blame to understanding, creating space for growth, empathy, and resolution.

A Lesson from Football: Letting Go in Competition

I vividly recall a football match during my late teenage years. As a center-back, my role was to defend aggressively, and my actions frustrated the opposing players. I tackled them, blocked their passes, and denied them goals. The match was intense, and emotions ran high, but once the final whistle blew, the atmosphere transformed.

Despite the challenges on the field, everyone shook hands with smiles. Why? Because we all adopted a wider perspective.

Here's how this perspective unfolded during and after the match:

- **Normalizing Conflict**: Players understood that intensity is inherent to football. This realization diffused anger, as the aggression was seen as part of the game rather than a personal attack.
- **Self-Reflection**: The opposing team likely recognized their own shortcomings—be it a lack of skill, speed, or strategy—that contributed to their struggles. This motivated them to improve rather than hold grudges.
- **Appreciating Effort**: Each team acknowledged the hard work and determination of the other. This mutual respect fostered sportsmanship and companionship.

The Three Steps to Letting Go of Grudges

1. Normalize the Situation
Understand that conflict and disagreements are a natural part of life. Whether in sports, relationships, or the workplace, clashes are inevitable when individuals with different goals, values, or expectations interact.

2. Reflect and Learn
Ask yourself:

- What can I learn from this situation?
- Did I contribute to the conflict? If so, how?
- How can I use this experience to grow?

Reflection transforms grudges into opportunities for self-improvement.

3. Practice Forgiveness
Forgiveness doesn't mean condoning harmful behavior; it means freeing yourself from the emotional weight of resentment. When you forgive, you regain control over your thoughts and emotions, creating space for peace and positivity.

Why Grudges Are Negotiable

Holding grudges consumes mental and emotional energy, leaving less room for joy, creativity, and growth. By choosing to negotiate and release these feelings, we:

- Strengthen our relationships.
- Improve our mental health.
- Foster a sense of inner peace.

The wider perspective is a powerful tool in this process. It allows us to see the humanity in others, recognize our shared imperfections, and embrace forgiveness as a path to freedom.

Conclusion

Grudges are negotiable because they are born of perspective, and perspectives can change. By normalizing conflicts, reflecting on our role in them, and practicing forgiveness, we can release the burden of resentment and move forward with clarity and compassion.

Life is too short to hold onto grudges. Let them go, embrace a wider perspective, and watch how your relationships and inner peace flourish.

Chapter- 14

Motivation and Discipline

The Role of Motivation and Discipline in the Life of an Individual

Motivation and discipline are two pillars that support an individual in achieving their goals, overcoming challenges, and thriving in both personal and professional life. Their importance becomes particularly evident during difficult times, as I experienced when facing a severe back injury that tested my physical, emotional, and mental strength. Let me share my journey and how these two principles shaped my recovery and growth.

The Incident: A Life-Altering Injury

One day, during a football match, I jumped high to win a header and clear the ball from our final third. The opponent also leaped but couldn't win the duel, resorting to fouling me instead. This unfortunate clash led to a lower back injury that forced me to leave the field. Later, I was diagnosed with lower back inflammation, requiring at least a year of rest.

At the time, I was working full-time as a video editor, a job that demanded prolonged sitting and intense focus. With me out of action, both my football and office teams suffered, and they had to make significant compromises to cope with my absence. This situation was not only physically painful but also emotionally and mentally draining.

The Recovery Journey

A few weeks later, I began physiotherapy to strengthen my back. My therapist worked tirelessly with me, but the process was grueling. I had never faced such a debilitating injury before, and the fear of losing my football career loomed large. Many colleagues and relatives doubted my ability to recover fully, let alone return to the sport. Despite these doubts, I managed to defy expectations and recover in just seven months.

However, this recovery wasn't just about the external efforts like physiotherapy; it was driven by an internal process that combined motivation, discipline, and self-belief. Let me share the key components of this internal process.

Internal Process: The Hidden Engine of Recovery

1. Meditation

During my recovery, I turned to meditation. It became a tool to keep my mind free from negativity and fear. Meditation helped me maintain mental clarity and focus on what truly mattered: my healing and future goals. It created a space where I could visualize success and stay calm despite the challenges.

2. Reading

Books became my refuge and a source of inspiration. Reading allowed me to immerse myself in stories of resilience and growth, providing valuable lessons and keeping my inner fire alive. It was one of the most effective ways to stay mentally engaged and motivated.

3. Writing

Writing played a crucial role in my recovery. As I've shared in the chapter "The Five W's," writing helps connect with one's thoughts. During this period, I journaled extensively, reflecting on both positive and negative emotions. This practice helped me process my experiences and make sense of the journey.

4. Overtime Work

Recovery required extra effort—both mentally and physically. Drawing from my previous experience of working overtime in the office, I applied the same principle to my physiotherapy. If my therapist recommended three repetitions of an exercise, I'd push myself to do four. This extra effort accelerated my progress and boosted my confidence.

5. Avoiding Distractions

Friends and relatives often shared unsolicited advice, some of which was unhelpful or even counterproductive. I adhered to a simple rule: "Don't listen to the surroundings; listen to your inner voice." This mindset helped me filter out distractions and focus solely on my recovery.

6. Visualization

Even when I couldn't train on the field, I practiced mentally. I watched football matches and listened to podcasts to stay connected to the game. Through visualization, I imagined myself playing, honing my skills, and strategizing. This mental practice kept my football instincts sharp.

7. Ultimate Aim

Throughout my journey, I remained focused on one ultimate goal: returning to the football field stronger than ever. This unwavering focus was my guiding light, ensuring that I stayed on track despite doubts and setbacks.

Conclusion: The Power of Motivation and Discipline

Recovering from my back injury was a transformative experience. It taught me that motivation provides the spark to begin a journey, while discipline ensures you stay on the path, even when the journey becomes arduous. Together, they create a powerful synergy that can help overcome any obstacle.

By meditating, reading, writing, working overtime, avoiding distractions, visualizing success, and maintaining a clear aim, I not only recovered but also grew stronger, both physically and mentally. This experience reinforced my belief in the power of internal processes and the importance of believing in oneself.

To anyone facing challenges, remember: the combination of motivation and discipline can help you conquer even the toughest battles. Stay focused, stay committed, and trust the process—success will follow you.

Additional Tips-

1. Start Your Day with Purpose

The way you start your morning sets the tone for the rest of the day. Dedicate the first 10–15 minutes to a simple routine that grounds you:

- Stretch or meditate to center your thoughts.
- Write down your top three priorities for the day.
- Reflect on an affirmation like, *"I am capable of achieving my goals today."*
  This practice cultivates clarity and motivation right from the start.

---

2. Embrace the Power of Small Wins

Small achievements add up to significant progress. Break your larger goals into smaller, manageable tasks, and celebrate every step forward. For instance, if you aim to write a book, commit to drafting just one paragraph a day.

Why It Works: Small victories release dopamine, the brain's "reward chemical," keeping you motivated and consistent.

---

3. Practice the 2-Minute Rule

If something takes less than two minutes to complete, do it immediately. Tasks like replying to an email, tidying up your desk, or filing paperwork become less daunting when handled promptly. This habit keeps your to-do list manageable and prevents procrastination.

---

4. Develop a Power Routine

Your daily habits define your life. Create a set of simple but impactful routines:

- Exercise for 20 minutes.
- Read or learn something new for 15 minutes.
- Review and adjust your goals for the day.

These small, consistent actions ensure steady progress and balance.

---

5. Cultivate Gratitude Daily

Gratitude shifts your focus from what's missing to what you have. Each evening, write down three things you're grateful for, no matter how small they seem. Gratitude fosters positivity and improves mental well-being.

Example:

- "I'm grateful for the kind smile I received today."
- "I'm grateful for finishing my work on time."

---

6. The Rule of Reflection

Spend five minutes at the end of your day reflecting on what went well and what could be improved. This practice helps you identify patterns, learn from mistakes, and prepare for tomorrow with a clear mind.

---

7. Learn to Declutter

A cluttered space often leads to a cluttered mind. Dedicate time each week to organize your workspace, home, or even your digital devices. Decluttering creates a sense of control and fosters creativity.

---

8. Practice Visualization

Visualization is a powerful tool for achieving goals. Spend a few minutes each day imagining yourself succeeding—whether it's acing a presentation or completing a challenging project. Picture the details: how it feels, looks, and even sounds.

Why It Works: The brain often doesn't distinguish between imagined and real experiences, making visualization an effective way to build confidence and focus.

---

9. Use the "5x5 Rule"

Ask yourself: *"Will this matter in 5 years? 5 months?"* If the answer is no, let it go. This helps you prioritize what's truly important and reduces unnecessary stress.

---

10. Stay Curious

Curiosity fuels growth. Commit to learning something new each day—whether it's reading an article, listening to a podcast, or trying a new skill. This keeps your mind sharp and opens doors to new opportunities.

---

11. Schedule Rest

Rest isn't laziness; it's necessary. Plan breaks throughout your day to recharge. Whether it's a 10-minute walk, a quick nap, or a moment of mindfulness, rest prevents burnout and boosts productivity.

---

12. Surround Yourself with Positivity

Your environment greatly influences your mindset. Spend time with people who uplift and inspire you, and distance yourself from negativity. Surround yourself with books, music, or even décor that motivates you.

---

13. Practice Kindness

Small acts of kindness can create ripple effects of positivity. Compliment someone, lend a helping hand, or simply listen when someone needs to talk. These actions not only benefit others but also enhance your own sense of fulfillment.

---

14. Adapt and Grow

Life is full of unexpected changes. Instead of resisting, embrace them. Adaptability is key to thriving in new circumstances. Use each challenge as an opportunity to learn and grow.

---

15. Stay Consistent

Consistency is the secret ingredient to success. Even when motivation wanes, stick to your habits. Remember, small daily actions lead to significant long-term results.

Final Thought:
These tips aren't just about achieving goals—they're about creating a life of balance, purpose, and happiness. Implementing even a few of these practices can transform how you approach your days, helping you find clarity amidst chaos and joy in every moment.

Acknowledgement

This book, *"Win Life in 100 Pages,"* is a culmination of my life's experiences, lessons, and the invaluable support of countless people.

First and foremost, I thank my family for their unwavering love and encouragement, especially my mother, whose wisdom continues to guide me every day. I am deeply grateful to my friends, mentors, and colleagues who inspired and motivated me to embark on this journey of self-discovery.

A special thanks to my readers, who have made this journey meaningful. Your belief in my words and stories encourages me to keep writing and sharing. To those who have shared their stories and struggles with me, thank you for trusting me. This book is for you and because of you.

Finally, I thank the challenges I faced, for they became my greatest teachers. To life, for teaching me the value of resilience, perseverance, and positivity.

This is just the beginning of a greater journey. Thank you for walking this path with me.